THE SENSUS COMMUNIS, SYNESTHESIA, AND THE SOUL

THE SENSUS COMMUNIS, SYNESTHESIA, AND THE SOUL

AN ODYSSEY

ERIC McLUHAN

McLuhan Institute Books

Assembly Press
PRINCE EDWARD COUNTY, ONTARIO

Copyright © 2015, 2025 Eric McLuhan
Introduction copyright © 2025 Luke Burgis

All rights reserved. This book is copyright material and no part of it may be copied, reproduced, transferred, distributed, leased, licensed, or publicly performed or used in any way except as specifically permitted in writing by the publisher, or a licence from Access Copyright, as allowed under the terms and conditions under which it was purchased or as strictly permitted by applicable copyright law.

Library and Archives Canada Cataloguing in Publication

Title: The sensus communis, synesthesia, and the soul : an odyssey / Eric McLuhan ; introduction by Luke Burgis.

Names: McLuhan, Eric, author | Burgis, Luke, writer of introduction
Description: Includes bibliographical references.

Identifiers: Canadiana (print) 20250165465 | Canadiana (ebook) 20250168898 | ISBN 9781998336050 (softcover) | ISBN 9781998336067 (EPUB)

Subjects: LCSH: Religion—Philosophy. | LCSH: Knowledge, Theory of (Religion) | LCSH: Communication—Religious aspects—Catholic Church. | LCSH: Digital media—Religious aspects—Catholic Church.

Classification: LCC BL51 .M243 2025 | DDC 210—dc23

Published by Assembly Press | assemblypress.ca

Cover and interior designed by Greg Tabor
Edited by Andrew McLuhan for McLuhan Institute Books

Printed and bound in Canada on uncoated paper made from 100% recycled content in line with our commitment to ethical business practices and sustainability.

To Dr. Steven Miller, for encouragement and assistance in publishing this essay

CONTENTS

Introduction Is Induction • 1
Foreword Is Forearmed • 9

Faith • 13
Synesthesia • 56
Becoming Discarnate • 75
Religion • 129

Appendices
One: Aristotle's Media War • 133
Two: Communication Arts in the Ancient World • 140
Three: Paradoxes of the Mass Audience • 143
Four: Literacies • 149
Five: Effects of the Discarnate • 157
Six: The Blindfold Exercise • 161
Seven: A Catholic Theory of Communication • 175
Eight: The Future of Humanity, Etc. • 189

(Happily Ever) Afterword • 195
Bibliography • 199

INTRODUCTION IS INDUCTION

IN OUR ELECTRONIC AGE, it's easy to fool and to be fooled. Trust in media and institutions is disintegrating, and many of us feel disoriented, finding it difficult to perceive the truth of things. That is because our organs of perception have been under attack for years—and these organs have become sclerotic in people who engage with media uncritically. It is as if, having binged on fast food for years, we have lost the ability to taste a good wine, or a bad wine, and to know which is which. Common sense has become uncommon. And yet it seems like it should be abundant—it is called common, after all.

At a time when our attention is scattered by screens and our senses scrambled by the cacophony of media, Eric McLuhan dares us to rediscover a deeper harmony of perception—a harmony that unites the body, intellect, and spirit. He breaks new ground by weaving insights about communications into a unified theory of the senses and their role in human experience—particularly religious experience. This short book is an exploration into the heart of what it means to be human, a journey toward recovering the lost art of soulcraft. It has done more to help me understand the modern challenge of both communicating and receiving truth than any other book written so far in the twenty-first century.

McLuhan dedicated his life to continuing the groundbreaking work of his father, Marshall McLuhan, to understand media and, through it, to rediscover new depths of human experience. Marshall once said that he "didn't think it was worthwhile to say anything unless it was controversial." The reader of today must be made to feel as if he's in a foreign land; he must be stirred and shaken and have his perception pricked so that he might see something beyond the normal hues, something beyond the frames which he has been habituated to. And so it makes sense that *The Sensus Communis, Synesthesia, and the Soul* appears to be a strange text. Especially because Eric, like Marshall, was a multidisciplinary thinker who applied his insights deftly across many domains. *The Sensus Communis* disjoints the reader, leaving one wondering what the "form" of the writing is. Is it a book? An essay? A collection of notes? Upon one's first reading it is hard to say. Eric McLuhan acknowledges the strangeness and answers the question about its form at the end. In the meantime, he allows you to feel defamiliarized by design. Standard forms are lulling us to sleep and this text—an odyssey—requires the reader to become dislocated, to experience it in order to understand.

The deepest form of knowing requires what Eric McLuhan refers to as a *sensus communis*, or common sense. In the modern world, the fragmentation of the senses makes it difficult to grasp the whole. This leaves us disjointed, extended in different places, in a rapidly disincarnating world. It has contributed to what my colleague Jon Askonas has called a post-consensus reality. It seems as if nobody is even seeing the same things.

Understanding how we got here, and how we can live well in a world like this, is a matter of urgent importance.

All of us are familiar with the five bodily senses of sight, sound, taste, touch, and smell. As McLuhan notes, there are also *intellectual senses* that correspond to both our exterior and interior worlds. When reading scripture, for instance (this book takes scriptural interpretation as its starting point), the literal or historical sense of the text anchors our interpretation of the text in reality—it conveys what the human author intended to communicate based on the historical, cultural, and linguistic context of the time. The Israelites, under Moses's leadership, crossed the Red Sea to flee from Pharaoh's army. The allegorical sense enables us to discern meaningful connections, such as seeing the crossing of the Red Sea as a type of baptism that symbolizes liberation, adding to the narrative's spiritual depth.

There are also moral and anagogical senses, which allow us to understand how the scripture is living and active, and how to encounter it. In the moral sense, the story of leaving Egypt and crossing the Red Sea challenges us to reflect on our own journey: What is the "Egypt" in my life—those forces of sin or oppression—that I must leave behind? Anagogically, crossing the Red Sea points to an ultimate destiny: just as the Israelites journeyed toward the Promised Land, I am on a pilgrimage through this world. The eschatological meaning of my journey is revealed to me. By engaging all four senses, scripture becomes not just a story or a lesson but a nexus of meaning and real encounter.

Eric McLuhan goes on to take us even deeper. He notes that there are also spiritual senses—faith, hope, and love—each having its own *sensus communis*, or locus of sense-making, which provides a way of knowing reality. Faith, according to McLuhan, is a "supernatural, experiential knowing of supernatural matters," a form of unmediated contact with ultimate things. Likewise, hope and love provide their own form of knowing the metaphysical. Together, the spiritual senses provide a knowledge of God so that we may see "through a glass, darkly" in this life—but see nonetheless.

Each of these three areas of sensory perception—the corporal, intellectual, and spiritual—has its own *sensus communis*. In the pages that follow, Eric McLuhan shows how deeply the different three primary domains of senses are interrelated to form an even richer *sensus communis*. When operating together, they provide a person with a single, unified experience of reality that is not fragmented or stunted. The result is a mode of being rarely experienced in our world today.

One person who seemed to experience reality with a fully active common sense is the blind French resistance fighter Jacques Lusseyran. When Lusseyran was seven, he was blinded in a schoolyard accident. Later in life, he wrote a memoir about how he regained his sight—not optical sight, but a form of seeing in which everything was "bathed in light." It allowed him to grasp the essence of things through an unmediated, faith-like knowing. He perceived interior realities without being able to see the exterior of things. He grew amused at the descriptions of the clothes people wore, because they rarely corresponded to the interior reality that he had gained the ability to see.

"Immediately, the substance of the universe drew together," Lusseyran writes in his autobiography, *And There Was Light*. "I was aware of a radiance emanating from a place I knew nothing about, a place which might as well have been outside me as within." Lusseyran seemed to have developed what modern psychologists call synesthesia, a condition in which people "taste shapes" or "see sounds," and other apparent paradoxes of perception—which is closer, McLuhan argues, to what the human experience might be like if we possessed a fully developed *sensus communis*.

The phenomenon of synesthesia began to fascinate Eric McLuhan soon after he learned about it. We might be able to understand the effects of modern media and technology by understanding how it prevents the *sensus communis* from ever occurring in the vast majority of people. Is synesthesia our birthright, a way of reclaiming the *sensus communis*?

To understand this question, we must turn to the question of *mimesis*. I first read *The Sensus Communis, Synesthesia, and the Soul* at the recommendation of Andrew McLuhan, Eric's son. I had just published a book, *Wanting: The Power of Mimetic Desire in Everyday Life*, about the ways in which *mimesis* shapes what we want. The concept of *mimesis*, according to the French thinker René Girard, refers to the subconscious and often hidden forms of imitation that humans engage in constantly. We take cues from other people, even when it comes to our desires and sense of identity. *Mimesis* lets us participate in others' lives, fostering communion of the senses, and ultimately of desires, which can be healthy or unhealthy. *Mimesis* is ultimately about a form of social fusion that can distort our perception of reality. And because the primary subject of *The Sensus Communis* is the fusion of the senses, it is no surprise that *mimesis* has a central role to play.

There has been a long-standing debate in philosophy, going back at least to Plato, about the relationship between *mimesis* and truth. Plato thought that *mimesis* was dangerous, and he waged the first media war against the poets because he believed they encouraged a type of pre-rational, unmediated experience of reality that he thought was unequivocally bad. The poets and playwrights performed their works so that the distinction between actors and audience collapsed. The viewer became one with the performance through a mode of participation that Plato called *mimesis*: that is, a mode of participation that led to interiorization, a putting-on of something so as to become it.

As an alternative to *mimesis*, Plato preferred writing and logic, which help to keep the powerful forces of *mimesis* from consuming a person. To paraphrase the nineteenth century personalist John Henry Newman: no one's heart is inflamed by a syllogism, and no one loses themself in the cold logic of the textbook; it is concrete persons who captivate us in the fullness of our sensory experience. That is why the move away from orality and toward the written word was, for Plato, a step in the right direction: it stripped *mimesis* of its power over us by making it harder for us to get swept up in the action.

Plato was partly right. *Mimesis* is dangerous if we allow ourselves to be fused with evil or base things. *Mimesis* is dangerous when it leads to the loss of self-possession, which may explain why it is so easy to fool and to be fooled these days—perhaps we live during the greatest spike of *mimesis* the world has ever seen, with social media fusing people together in ways they can scarcely understand, unable to know where one person or thing ends and another begins. Yet *mimesis* is also the pathway to communion. Saint Paul says to put on Christ. *Mimesis* is the process through which a person comes to total identification, complete communion, with Jesus, which is the goal of the spiritual life for a Christian. This positive sense of *mimesis* should be recovered in its full depth, as Paul and Eric McLuhan both understood.

The deepest reading of scripture requires *mimesis*, or

communion with the text through lived experience. The sacramental life too invites people to a deep form of *mimesis*—that is, communion with spiritual realities. The communion happens through participation at the level of the *sensus communis*. If a person's senses are totally fragmented or dulled, how could they understand the mystery of the Eucharist? The sacrament appears as bread and wine—but faith, hope, and love reveal its reality. Thomas Aquinas, in his hymn to the Eucharist, still sung during Eucharistic adoration in Catholic churches across the world today, gave Eric McLuhan the greatest support for his thesis: "may faith supply a supplement for the defect of the senses."

The sacraments transform us. But not only that: they are mysteries that develop the *sensus communis* in us in the first place. The fundamental massage that I have received from this book has limbered me up to see that the sacraments, which are visible signs of invisible realities, are the key to understanding communication at its most profound level.[1]

Eric McLuhan himself described this work as a "prologue" or "set of notes" to a larger and deeper exploration he hoped others, especially theologians, might continue. Its urgency lies in the task it presents: to restore a sense of wholeness in a world increasingly fragmented by the forces of modern media. "The world is charged with the grandeur of God," wrote Gerard Manley Hopkins. To the extent that we develop the organ of common sense, our lives will become charged to meet it.

Luke Burgis
Feast of the Immaculate Conception, 2024

Note

1   See *The Medium is the Massage: An Inventory of Effects*, written by Marshall McLuhan and illustrated by Quintin Fiore, published in 1967.

FOREWORD IS FOREWARNED

WHEN I CAME ACROSS a description of the experience of mysticism in Henri de Lubac's magisterial *Medieval Exegesis: The Four Senses of Scripture,* I found myself on familiar ground. It brought forcefully to mind the experience of *mimesis* in ancient Greek poetics.

> *Mimesis* is the technique of interiorization: knowing by putting-on, knowing by becoming, intellectually and emotionally, the thing known. That is, integral, interiorized knowing instead of conceptual knowing: *unmediated, direct perception* by the body and the emotions and the intellect of the hearer, that is, by the hearer's soul. Direct experience by total submergence. (p. 27, *infra.*)

Fifty years ago, Eric Havelock wrote in *Preface to Plato* about Plato's "war" with the bards over their use of *mimesis.* Their approach engendered the total, the almost pathological involvement of the hearer in the poetic performance, an involvement so profound that the hearer effectively became the poem. He put on the characters; he spoke their words; he performed their actions; he suffered, triumphed, exulted, despaired as they did, and he did this so completely that a single exposure would fix the recitation perfectly in his memory for the rest of his life.

> Thirty years later you could automatically quote what Achilles had said or what the poet had said about him. Such enormous powers of poetic memorization could be purchased only at the cost of total loss of objectivity... This then is the master clue to Plato's choice of the word *mimesis* to describe the poetic experience. It focuses initially not on the artist's creative act but on his power to make his audience identify almost pathologically and certainly sympathetically with the content if what he is saying... (p. 28, *infra*.)

Plato was determined to break the spell and inculcate instead the exotic new skills of abstract thought and objectivity that accompanied the alphabet. Abstraction was essential to the new science of philosophy, so Plato waged the first media war. Aristotle continued the campaign with an immensely powerful technology of his own devising: the syllogism.

Fifteen hundred years after Plato and Aristotle, as de Lubac reveals, *mimesis* can again be found at work, albeit in a totally separate context, that of the interpretation of Scripture. More particularly, interpretation at the level of mysticism, the "anagogical" level. Unlike the historical, allegorical, and tropological senses of Scripture, the anagogical sense does not consist of ideas: it is constituted as direct experience, one generally regarded as ineffable and beyond words or explanation. The reader puts on, or enters into, the passage of Scripture so completely as to become it. He transcends mere intellectual understanding and attains, through contemplation, a state of knowing through his whole being.

Perhaps equally surprising, *mimesis* is everywhere in evidence in our contemporary world, particularly in the arts and in advertising, and in modern media. This reversal has implications for the Church and the sacraments, implications that need to be addressed without delay.

Accordingly, this essay concerns both experience and the several kinds of sense: intellectual, corporeal, and spiritual. As far as possible I have tried to avoid theory and stick to a common sense approach. Moreover, the ancient and medieval doctrine of common sense, the human *sensus communis*, is particularly relevant to contemporary experience. It is evident for example in the condition psychologists call synesthesia, which also has much to tell us about *mimesis*.

These pages, then, treat the four senses of exegesis mentioned above (and particularly anagogy), and the bodily senses, and *mimesis* as experiences and as modes of insight, and not in terms of ideas or theories. Experiences can be checked, shared, verified by anyone. These considerations naturally bring into the discussion the notion of the common sense, which today plays such a central part in the study of communication and the associated technologies. In turn, the *sensus communis*, an obscure artifact of Aristotelian philosophy and medieval theology, has quietly invaded the unsuspecting contemporary world disguised as *synesthesia*. And the poets, and the blind, have much to offer us on its account, so they contribute a few insights to our discussion. The senses we discuss are multifarious: there are the five bodily senses, and the intellectual senses of Scripture that de Lubac discusses, and also the theological senses (the theological virtues of faith, hope, charity), and each group, we discover, has its own *sensus communis*, and the three groups are in communion with one another.

Modern media exert a profound and destabilizing effect on the *sensus communis* and on the interrelation of the various senses; consequently, we turn in these pages to a consideration of the importance and significance of the body. The meaning of the human body cannot be overstated, as John Paul II shows in depth in his seminal *Man and Woman He Created Them: A Theology of the Body*: the body is everywhere assaulted by all of our new media, a state that has resulted in deep disorientation of intellect and destabilization of culture throughout the world. In the age of disembodied communication, the meaning and significance and experience of the body are utterly transformed and distorted.

Before we can take steps to counteract the influence of our technologies on our senses, we must investigate how they bring their influence to bear and what can be done about that. On the one hand, the arts may hold a significant part of the answer; on the other, an increased emphasis on participation in the sacraments would go a long way toward rectifying matters.

It is time to bring forward a Catholic theory of communication[2] that takes into account the transformation of the users of media.

Eric McLuhan
Bloomfield, Ontario, 2013–2015

Note

2   See Appendix Seven, *infra*.

FAITH

"Anyone wishing to follow reason alone would be a confirmed lunatic in the opinion of the greater part of the world" (Pascal). Anyone wishing to follow faith alone is liable to be a confirmed heretic for many people—so little do the standards of judgment of many men, seemingly the most jealous of orthodoxy, partake of the order of faith.

Anyone wishing, in what concerns faith, to be guided by faith alone, must in any case be prepared to walk alone.

But his solitude is only apparent. It is a solitude filled with invisible presences. It is the painful condition of the deepest and purest communion.

—Henri de Lubac, *Paradoxes of Faith*

FAITH IS A GIFT of the Holy Spirit,[3] that is, a kind of revelation. St. Thomas wrote, "faith must needs be from God. Because those things which are of faith surpass human reason, hence they do not come to man's knowledge, unless God reveal them. To some, indeed, they are revealed by God immediately, as those things which were revealed to the apostles and prophets…"[4] Faith, then, provides knowledge.

> The starting point of Christian experience is faith. Faith is not replaced by experience, but it remains the comprehensive form of Christian experience. This is the first point to be made about Christian experience, as Wojtyla understands it: its origin and measure lies in faith, not the other way around. Faith must be "enriched," that is, it must become more mature and conscious, able to form the whole of experience. "Faith and the enrichment of faith is a supernatural gift from God and is not subject to human planning or causation; but man, and the Church as a human community, can and must cooperate with the grace of faith and contribute to its enrichment."[5, 6]

I have always understood faith to be "a way of knowing": another sense, not one of touch & co., but nonetheless one by which you simply *know* certain things, analogous to how you *know* that something is coarse or smooth, or loud, or bright, or sweet, or stinks.

Faith, then, is not opinion, and it is not belief (in the common, loose sense), though we often use these terms casually to refer to it. Belief and opinion are things we decide to have. "Believe" can mean several things. At one end of the spectrum there is "I believe that it will rain tomorrow." And also "I believe that astronauts *did* land on the moon, and that nobody faked the whole thing in the Arizona desert." At the other end there is the "believe" in "Credo in unum deum, patrem omnipotentem…"

which is decidedly close to the idea of faith, if not synonymous with it. Still, faith is not a decision but a knowing, a kind of perception and knowledge given to or through the soul; it uses the soul as a sense modality, a medium of communication. "Only faith enables us to experience the salvific presence of God in Christ in the very center of life and of history. Faith alone reveals to us the meaning of the human condition and our supreme dignity as sons and daughters of God who are called to communion with him."[7] Faith is supernatural, *experiential* knowing of supernatural matters.

St. Paul wrote that "faith is the substance of things hoped for, the evidence of things unknown" (Hebrews 11:1). St. Paul was not waxing metaphorical here: he meant these statements to be taken at face value. A substance does not consist of opinion or belief: you can experience it. Equally with evidences: you may have opinions about them, and you may express belief or incredulity or doubt about them, as with any experience, but neither belief nor opinion is faith. They aren't knowledge.

So faith is *unmediated* (that is, it circumvents the bodily senses), *direct knowledge* of things spiritual. Anagogical *knowledge*. Henri de Lubac approaches the matter circuitously:

> The divinity of the Word of God incarnate is in fact the central object of allegory. It is revealed, however, only to the "eyes of the heart," to those "inner eyes," those "spiritual eyes, those "eyes of the soul," those "better eyes," that are opposed to the eyes of the flesh and which are in reality the eyes received from God, the eyes "illuminated by the Gospel" or, following a frequent expression, the "eyes of the faith." For *faith has her own eyes*. Faith is the light

"that makes one see the light of the spirit in the law of the letter"; it is like a lamp lit in the night, penetrating the thick cloud of all the biblical "sacraments" which surround it. We are therefore to be imbued in the faith through allegory. The truths of the allegory, "mysteries of Christ and the Church," are the "mysteries of the faith" hidden in the ceremonies of the law." They are the "sacraments of our faith."[8]

De Lubac points out that allegory is the doctrinal sense *par excellence*, and observes (p. 109), "One can therefore define the Christian faith as 'allegorica doctrina.' In fact, 'what is allegory but the mystic doctrine of the mysteries?'[9] Its content is exactly 'the doctrine of the holy Church.'"[10] And he adds, "This relation of the faith to allegory, as always when it is a question of effecting passage to a higher order, can be understood only as a relation of reciprocal causality."[11] A few lines later, he reiterates:

> But in reality, let us say it again, there is essentially no point to look for any priority of allegory received by relation to faith nor of faith received by relation to the perception of allegory: each mutually conditions the other. It is one and the same indivisible act—the elements and logical instants of which later theology will analyze—that gives access to the one and to the other under the action of the Spirit of Christ.[12]

For centuries, the various senses of Scripture were grouped as the literal (or historical) sense and the allegorical sense.

Gradually, the latter term came to refer to an allegorical understanding of the literal sense, and the word "tropology" came to refer to two senses distinct from the allegorical sense, the moral and anagogical senses.

No more than *allegoria* for the second sense was the word *tropologia* imposed here. In the most general acceptation, a trope was a figure, a mode, or a turn of phrase (Greek, *tropos*, Latin *conversio*), by which one turns some expression to designate some object other than the one naturally meant.[13] Tropologia, accordingly, was a speech turned around or "turning" something else "around"; it was a "turned" or "turning" manner of speech. There was nothing in it that might suggest an idea of moral conversion—any more than there was in *allegoria* anything that would suggest the mystery of Christ. Thus we understand that, within the nascent vocabulary of exegesis, "tropology" at first had been practically synonymous with allegory, as well as with anagogy. The process that little by little needed to distinguish and specialize these three words was almost entirely contingent. *Allegoria* was found to have a right of priority, chiefly because of Saint Paul; it therefore designated, prior to every other distinction, the collection of senses added to *historia*, then, more precisely, the first among them, which in a certain fashion stood at the head of the other two. Anagogy belonged naturally enough to the fourth. All that remained for tropology, then, was the third place; it took it and kept it. It was even more natural that the only figured sense, already designated by this word, would, among the pre-Christian exegetes of the Bible, be found practically to be the moral sense. Then it would be explained as being "a speech turned around toward us, i.e., toward our ways of behaving," or "a speech turning around, pertaining to the mind's ways of behaving."[14]

The literal sense of Scripture, also called the historical sense, "contains" all of the other senses inasmuch as, without the letters (*litterae*), there is no Scripture at all, just blank sheets of paper. But that is not the intended meaning of the term. "Literal" refers, first of all, to the written *littera*, the letter[15] on the page. Letters, words, sentences present the historical narrative: the narrative contains three other senses of Scripture and is the *sine qua non* of Scripture and interpretation. I would prefer to separate the terms "literal" and "historical" rather than continue to use them interchangeably.

But to return: *Littera gesta docet,* runs the old verse. The next line positions the role of allegory: *Quid credas allegoria*. Then comes the tropological turn:

> Littera gesta docet,
> Quid credas allegoria;
> Moralis quid agas,
> Quo tendis anagogia.

The first two senses, literal/historical and allegorical, are outward, objective senses; the remaining two are interior, mystical senses. Comments de Lubac:

> [Tropology] occupies the third place in the most frequent and the most logical formulation of the four senses—and which even those who make no distinct mention of it did not miss—relates to the spiritual sense proper to Scripture, not only in fact but also by necessity. It contributes to the elaboration of this sense which characterizes Scripture only. It does not precede "the spiritual edifice," but it "adds to it," or rather it exerts itself within it to complete it. It is within allegory. It constitutes an integral part of the mystery. Coming after the objective aspect of which it is the allegory, it constitutes its subjective aspect. It is, if one can say so, its intussusception, its interiorization; it appropriates it for us. Tropology draws its exempla from this mysterium. It is this "mystic sense of morality,"[16] this "understanding of spiritual life," that a practiced eye detects everywhere in the two Testaments. If allegory, starting from the facts of history, envisions the mystical body in its head or in its totality, tropology envisions it in each of its members.[17]

"Everything," de Lubac points out, "is consummated in the inner man." He insists over and over that the interiorized experience of the Scriptures is not illusion but real experience, experience minus the bodily senses, that is, unmediated by the body; thus it is direct experience, which is also mystical experience, direct contact. How this is achieved remains to be seen, *infra*. "No more," he insists, is it

> a question of gratifying oneself intellectually in a knowledge of the mysteries of allegory that would

remain completely objective, leaving the heart unchanged. This would be an illusory knowledge; for in these sorts of things understanding comprehends nothing if experience is absent:[18] the mystery interiorizes itself within the heart, where it becomes experience[19]—though always passing over in itself "the limits of experience" as well as those of reason. The "virtus mysteriorum," their proper energy, acts within the one who contemplates them in faith.[20]

The moral sense and the anagogic sense are in continuity with each other; the object they aim at is of the same structure:[21] anagogy is the extension of mystical tropology.[22] Garnier of Rochefort, a disciple of both Origen and of Dionysus, as well as of St. Gregory and of John Scotus, describes anagogy in terms that are at the same time a description of ecstasy:

> ...Climbing to the heights by the steps of sure contemplation, the human mind also contemplates anagogically the heavenly secrets by the holy gaze of divine eloquence; and thus starting from two kinds of visions it ascends to all the perfection that had been infused in the minds of theologians and prophets through the grace of divine revelation; in Greek they call this (first) kind of revelation *theophanies*, i.e., divine manifestations; the other, whereby it strives to contemplate the most heavenly one as he is by the mind's climbing up and going out in nakedness and purity and without covering,[23] is the kind that is called anagogic.
>
> But in this last kind of vision the human so

trembles and shudders that, dizzied by the darkness of its own ignorance, it cannot go forth toward that brightness and glow of truth unless it be directed; but, as it were, blind and guided by hand, it advances whither it does not see and begins to be melted through the vision and the visitation of the Beloved, so that it neither conceives what it ought or wants to about God nor is able to utter what it conceives, when it strives to investigate that bit of the heavenly kingdom beyond still surrounded by veils and the yet uncircumscribed dimension of the divine glow, and, though still investigating, fails. Thunderstruck, the mind clings fast in contemplation; it becomes numb with agitation; speaking, it is rendered utterly silent; and the copiousness that poverty had made copious returns the poverty; in advancing it falls short in wondrous way, and then advances the more once it has reached its shortfall.[24]

De Lubac comments on the unity of the fourfold senses:

It is in traditional eschatology that the doctrine of the four senses is achieved and finds its unity. For Christianity is a fulfillment, but in this very fulfillment it is a promised hope. Mystical or doctrinal, taught or lived, true anagogy is therefore always eschatological. It stirs up the desire for eternity in us. This is also why the fourth sense is forced to be the last. No more than it could really lack the three others could it be followed by a fifth. Neither is hope ever lacking nor, in our earthly condition, is it ever surpassed even if it already encroaches upon its term.[25]

The exterior historical sense contains the other senses inasmuch as without the narrative there is nothing; the anagogic and tropological senses contain the others in an organic unity of interiorized experience. Together they are the *sensus communis* of the intellectual human soul. And that interiorized experience is characterized by incompleteness; it needs, it demands, human participation to complete it:

> *Mysterium Christi*. Only this unique mystery possesses infinite depths, and the mind of each of the faithful has varying capacities for comprehending it. From this there results for every spiritual understanding, as we have seen more especially for anagogy, an incurable character of incompleteness. But, as the Gregorian term *volatus* for anagogy has already indicated, this fatal incompleteness is to be considered above all in its positive and dynamic aspect. The Word of God does not cease to create and to hollow out within the one who readies himself for it the capacity to receive it, with the result that the faithful understanding can increase indefinitely. By allegory the old text can always let more novelty shine through;[26] the new mystery can always be more interiorized and introduce eternity more deeply into the heart.[27]

The poet Ezra Pound charmingly characterizes the process of meaning as "the dance of the intellect among the words."

The mysterious accomplishment of that mystical interiorization and completion comes about via the *sensus communis* of the body and has been practiced for millennia by the poets. The common sense that Aquinas discusses, the *sensus communis*, is itself an interior sense, the interior aspect of the sense of touch, of which all of the other bodily senses are extensions or articulations.[28] The common sense is as it were the etymology of each and every one of the exterior bodily senses, just as anagogy is as it were the etymology of each and every one of the other Scriptural senses. St. Thomas makes the same observation: "The interior sense is called 'common' not by predication, as if it were a genus; but as the common root and principle of the exterior senses."[29]

That is, the common sense is the "place" where the exterior ("proper") senses meet: it is identical with touch, for us the enveloping sense, the environment of the whole body.

> The proper sense judges of the proper sensible by discerning it from other things which come under the same sense; for instance by discerning white from black or green. But neither sight nor taste can discern white from sweet: because what discerns between two things must know both. Wherefore the discerning judgment must be assigned to the common sense; to which, as to a common term, all apprehensions of the senses must be referred: and by which, again, all the intentions of the senses are perceived; as when someone sees that he sees. For this cannot be done by the proper sense, which only knows the form of the sensible by which it is immuted, in which immutation the action of sight

is completed and from which immutation follows another in the common sense which perceives the act of vision.[30]

Touch, then, as all of the bodily senses at once, is the locus of what we call synesthesia;[31] equally, anagogy is the locus of intellectual synesthesia, the scriptural sense that is home to, and that consists of, all of the senses of Scripture taken together. Ergo, just as the bodily senses are particulars of the common sense of touch, so the other scriptural senses are particulars of the anagogical sense. The home of both modes of synesthesia is of course the human soul, that which animates the body and makes it human. There, the two modes of synesthesia are in active interface, active interchange.

Gilson argues that "there are not two conceivable solutions of the problem of knowledge, one for the [physical] senses, another for the intelligence":

> Sensible knowledge and intellectual knowledge can be, and indeed are, two different species or two different steps of the same kind of operation, so they rest inevitably upon a single explanation. If it were necessary to introduce an ideal cleavage in universal order, it would fall between the animal and the plant, not between the animal and man. Restrained as is its field of operation, the animal is still increased by the being of others through the sensation it experiences. It is, therefore, sharply, though still incompletely, disengaged from pure materiality.[32] Hence we have to explain cognitive operations in such a way that we can attach both

intelligence and sensation to the same principle and judge them by the same rules.[33]

We have five exterior senses: sight, hearing, taste, touch, smell; they are articulations of / divisions of tactility, the common sense.

Five is the number for expression, for the exterior world. The science of rhetoric has five divisions. Words are modes of experience,[34] and are themselves experiences; a language is an organ of perception (poetic knowledge).

Aquinas equates the common sense with the soul,[35] the "common" sense, meaning all of the senses at once. I now take this understanding to apply to the four inward senses: together they form a complementary kind of common sense.

It is essential to bear in mind that there are not two human souls, one inward and one outward, but one human soul with twin sensitivities. St. Thomas deals with this and the related matters in the *Summa Theologica* as follows:

> According to the Philosopher, *Metaphysics* VIII (Did. VII. 2), difference is derived from the form. But the difference which constitutes man is *rational*, which is applied to man on account of his intellectual principle. Therefore the intellectual principle is the form of man.[36]

Then the *Respondeo*:

> We must assert that the intellect which is the principle of intellectual operation is the form of the human body. For that whereby primarily anything

acts is a form of the thing to which the act is to be attributed: for instance, that whereby a body is primarily healed is health, and that whereby the soul knows primarily is knowledge; hence health is a form of the body and knowledge is a form of the soul and as life appears through various operations in different degrees of living things, that whereby we primarily perform each of all these vital actions is the soul. For the soul is the primary principle of our nourishment, sensation, and local movement; and likewise of our understanding. Therefore this principle by which we primarily understand, whether it be called the intellect or the intellectual soul, is the form of the body. This is the demonstration used by Aristotle (*De Anima*, II, 2)… it follows therefore that the intellectual principle is the proper form of man.[37]

Latin had no single word for the Greek word *logos*, so the phrase *ratio atque oratio* was used, and with this translation the alliance of Grammar (literary encyclopedism) and Rhetoric (transformation) was cemented. De Lubac positions Grammar as follows:

"The art of Donatus," indeed, that "fundamental discipline," "the origin and foundation of the liberal arts,"[38] was more than a simple technique concerned with language, more too than that "explication of the poets" about which Saint Isidore of Seville was still talking. In the form of culture that prevailed in the first middle age, as a result of a process to which Christianity was otherwise alien, the whole life of the mind develops, so to speak, under its sign. "Grammar" here has become a "tool of intellectual research,"[39] comprising the totality of the rules that govern discourse and thereby those that govern thought. "It is necessary," says a capitulary of Charlemagne, whose influence was immense, "to know the figures of words and thoughts to comprehend the mysteries of holy Scripture."[40] The discussion instituted about the *modi significandi* therefore extended, in fact, albeit in a still indirect manner, implicit or ill-perceived, to the *modi intelligendi*. The "science of speaking correctly" was close to the "science of speaking truly."[41] Under Grammar, "the most elaborated form of profane knowledge," logic was concealed,[42] and the latter was already heavy with metaphysics.[43]

The grammatical *logos*[44] (the *logos spermatikos*), on the one hand, has four divisions: the four senses of Scripture—historical, allegorical, moral, and anagogical—and, on the other hand, has four causes: formal, efficient, material, and final (for reading and interpreting the Book of Nature).

The soul is as it were a medium, so structured to accept, to house, the *logos* of faith. That the soul is the formal cause of the body can be realized by elimination: the soul is not the material cause of the body inasmuch as the soul is immaterial. It is not the final cause of the body. And it is not the efficient cause of the body.[45] In addition, consider these observations by Gilson:

The notion of soul is much wider than that of a human soul. In its wide sense soul is defined as the first act of an organized body capable of performing the functions of life. Thus, like all form, a soul is an act.[46]

For St. Thomas, following Aristotle, the soul does not first make a body move, it first makes it a body. A corpse is not a body. The soul makes it exist as a body. It is the soul which assembles and organizes what we call today the bio-chemical element… in order to make a living body from them. In this complete sense, the soul is its *first act*; that is, is what makes it to be.[47]

…Therefore human knowledge is the operation of a form which, insofar as it is fitted for knowing bodies, is essentially a stranger to all corporeity. Since the human soul performs operations in which the body has no part, it is a form in which the body has no part. To operate by itself it must subsist by itself, because being is the cause of operation, and everything acts according as it is. What subsists by itself is a substance. The human soul, therefore, is an immaterial substance.[48]

…The rational soul, as a substance, is not affected by the corruption of the body. Indeed the body only exists by the soul whereas the soul does not exist by the body.[49]

…That by which a being passes from potency to act is, indeed, the proper form and the act of this being. Now the living body is only alive in potency until the soul has come to inform it. Only while it is vivified and animated by its soul does the human body really deserve its name. The eye or the arm of a corpse is no more a real eye or arm than if painted on canvas or sculptured in stone. It is the soul that places the body into the species of human body. It is the soul that confers upon it in act the being it possesses. The soul, then, is really its form as we have supposed. Not only can we deduce this conclusion from a consideration of the human body which the soul animates and vivifies, but also from the definition of the human species. When we wish to find out the nature of a being, we have only to determine what its operation is. Now the proper operation of man, considered as man, is intellectual knowledge. Through it he surpasses in dignity all the other animals. It is for this reason that Aristotle places man's sovereign happiness in this characteristic operation. hence it is this principle of intellectual operation which puts man in the species in which he finds himself. But the species of a being is always determined by its proper form. Therefore the intellective principle, that is, the human soul, is the proper form of man.[50]

More recently, Pope John Paul II referred[51] to

> the Church's *teachings on the unity of the human person*, whose rational soul is *per se et essentialiter* [through itself and essentially] the form of his body. The spiritual and immortal soul is the principle of unity of the human being, whereby it exists as a

whole—*corpore et anima unus*—as a person. These definitions not only point out that the body, which has been promised the resurrection, will also share in glory. They also remind us that the reason and free will are linked with all the bodily and sense faculties. *The person, including the body, is completely entrusted to himself, and it is in the unity of body and soul that the person is the subject of his own moral acts.* The person, by the light of reason and the support of virtue, discovers in the body the anticipatory signs, the expression and the promise of the gift of self.[52]

The soul, the formal cause of the body, can exist without the body, though it does not preexist the body; but the body cannot exist without the soul. As the *ground* for the body, the soul makes the body human; it gives the body life. Accordingly, there are two states of the same soul/substance:

> It is insofar as it is an intellect that the human soul is an immaterial substance. However, remembering that the intellectual operation presupposes sensation and demands the collaboration of the body, St. Thomas says without hesitation that the intellect is the form of the human body: "We must assert that the intellect which is the principle of intellectual operation is the form of the human body."[53]

And there are two forms of common sense, one relating to the exterior experience of the body and one relating to the body's interior experience. The respective sciences are Grammar and Rhetoric.

Now, the medieval pattern of four senses of Scripture has its ancestry in a classical doctrine of philology that precedes Christianity, namely the four levels of exegesis of literature and of the Book of Nature, including man and society. Varro explains the four levels as follows:

> Now I shall set forth the origins of the individual words, of which there are four levels of explanation. The lowest is that to which even the common folk has come... The second is that to which old-time grammar has mounted, which shows how the poet has made each word which he has fashioned and derived...
>
> The third level is that to which philosophy ascended and on arrival began to reveal the nature of those words which are in common use... The fourth is that where the sanctuary is, and the mysteries of the high priest: if I shall not arrive at full understanding there, at any rate I shall cast about for a conjecture...[54]

While the multi-levelled exegesis of Scripture has been practiced continuously from the earliest days of the Church to the present, such "polysemous" compositions and interpretations among poets and critics have been relatively sporadic. Yet they have not died out but continue, even in our time. Dante Alighieri and T. S. Eliot are two of the better-known practitioners.

Throughout the Middle Ages, study of secular literature was cultivated in order to provide a training ground for the interpretation of scriptural texts. Interpretive skills were practiced first on Homer and Virgil and the poets, and then were applied to the Scriptures. But poets' use of the four senses of exegesis did not end with the advent of Christianity. Dante, a conspicuous example, composed his *Commedia* with polysemous interpretation in mind, as he explains in the celebrated letter to Lord Can Grande della Scala:

> For the clarification of what I am going to say, then, it should be understood that there is not just a single sense in this work: it might rather be called polysemous, that is, having several senses. For the first sense is that which is contained in the letter, while there is another which is contained in what is signified by the letter. The first is called literal, while the second is called allegorical, or moral or anagogical. And in order to make this manner of treatment clear, it can be applied to the following verses: "When Israel went out of Egypt, the house of Jacob from a barbarous people, Judea was made his sanctuary, Israel his dominion."[55] Now if we look at the letter alone, what is signified to us is the departure of the sons of Israel from Egypt during the time of Moses; if at the allegory, what is signified to us is our redemption through Christ; if at the moral sense, what is signified to us is the conversion of the soul from the sorrow and misery of sin to the state of grace; if at the anagogical, what is signified to us is the departure of the sanctified soul from bondage to the corruption of this world into the freedom of eternal glory. And although these mystical senses are called by various names, they may all be called allegorical, since they are all different

from the literal or historical. For allegory is derived from the Greek *alleon*, which means in Latin *alienus* ("belonging to another") or *diversus* ("different").

This being established, it is clear that the subject about which these two senses play must also be twofold. And thus it should first be noted what the subject of the work is when taken according to the letter, and then what its subject is when understood allegorically. The subject of the whole work, then, taken literally, is the state of soul after death, understood in a simple sense; for the movement of the whole work turns upon this and about this. If on the other hand the work is taken allegorically, the subject is man, in the exercise of his free will, earning or becoming liable to the rewards or punishments of justice.[56]

Now let us shift from the thirteenth century to the twentieth. T. S. Eliot composed his masterpiece, *Four Quartets*, by bringing together the inner *sensus communis* and the outer *sensus communis*, the whole consort dancing together in poetic synesthesia. Four tightly interlaced poems comprise the overall poem. Each of these four poems has five movements, patterned after the five divisions of rhetoric, *inventio, dispositio, elocutio, memoria,* and *pronuntiatio*.[57] The first of the constituent poems, "Burnt Norton," sets the scene as performing the historical level. It opens with:

> Time present and time past
> Are both perhaps present in time future,
> And time future contained in time past.

> If all time is eternally present
> All time is unredeemable.
> What might have been is an abstraction
> Remaining a perpetual possibility
> Only in a world of speculation.
> What might have been and what has been
> Point to one end, which is always present.
> Footfalls echo in the memory...

The second of the four sub-poems, "East Coker," performs the allegorical role in *Four Quartets*. It opens with:

> In my beginning is my end.[58] In succession
> Houses rise and fall, crumble, are extended,
> Are removed, destroyed, restored, or in their place
> In an open field, or a factory, or a by-pass.
> Old stone to new building, old timber to new fires,
> Old fires to ashes, and ashes to the earth
> Which is already flesh, fur and faeces,
> Bone of man and beast, cornstalk and leaf....

The next poem, "The Dry Salvages," puts on tropology:

> I do not know much about gods; but I think that the river
> Is a strong brown god—sullen, untamed and intractable,
> Patient to some degree, at first recognized as a frontier;
> Useful, untrustworthy, as a conveyor of commerce;
> Then only a problem confronting the builder of bridges.
> The problem once solved, the brown god is almost forgotten
> By the dwellers in cities—ever, however, implacable,
> Keeping his seasons and rages, destroyer, reminder

Of what men choose to forget....

Finally, "Little Gidding" performs the level of anagogy, the mystical world between inner and outer worlds; it begins:

> Midwinter spring is its own season
> Sempiternal though sodden towards sundown,
> Suspended in time, between pole and tropic.
> When the short day is brightest, with frost and fire,
> The brief sun flames the ice, on pond and ditches,
> In a windless cold that is the heart's heat,
> Reflecting in a watery mirror
> A glare that is blindness in the early afternoon.
> And glow more intense than blaze of branch or brazier,
> Stirs the dumb spirit: no wind but Pentecostal fire
> In the dark time of the year...

A major theme running throughout each of the four sub-poems is the intersection of time (and the timeless) and place (announced in the titles): "Burnt Norton," "East Coker," "The Dry Salvages," "Little Gidding"—each is a geographical locale. Further, each of the four constituent poems, each quartet, plays its themes on the same four basic instruments, such as places and elements (respectively air, earth, water, and fire), and seasons. It is the intersection of a particular space and time that transforms and purifies:

> To be conscious is not to be in time
> But only in time can the moment in the rose-garden...
> Be remembered; involved with past and future.

In Book I of *The Institutes of Oratory*, Quintilian sets out the program for eloquence, which includes the study of languages and the cultivation of both Grammar and Rhetoric:

> This profession may be most briefly considered under two heads, the art of speaking correctly and the interpretation of the poets; but there is more beneath the surface than meets the eye. For the art of writing is combined with that of speaking, and correct reading precedes interpretation, while in each of these cases criticism has its work to perform. Nor is it sufficient to have read the poets only; every kind of writer must be carefully studied, not merely for the subject matter, but for the vocabulary; for words often acquire authority from their use by a particular author. Nor can such training be regarded as complete if it stop short of music, for the teacher of literature has to speak of metre and rhythm: nor again if he be ignorant of astronomy, can he understand the poets; for they, to mention no further points, frequently give their indications of time by reference to the rising and setting of the stars. Ignorance of philosophy is an equal drawback.[59]

In Book III, following Cicero (who, in his turn, continued the program of Isocrates), he presents the divisions of rhetoric and their basic characters:

> The art of oratory, as taught by most authorities, and those the best, consists of five parts: *invention*,

> *arrangement, expression, memory,* and *delivery* or *action* (the two latter terms being used synonymously). But all speech expressive of purpose involves also a subject and words. If such expression is brief and contained within the limits of one sentence, it may demand nothing more, but longer speeches require much more. For not only what we say and how we say it is of importance, but also the circumstances under which we say it. It is here that the need of arrangement comes in. But it will be impossible to say everything demanded by the subject, putting each thing in its proper place, without the aid of memory. It is for this reason that memory forms the fourth department. But a delivery, which is rendered unbecoming either by voice or gesture, spoils everything and almost entirely destroys the effect of what is said. Delivery therefore must be assigned the fifth place.[60]

Both patterns are synchronic and simultaneous rather than diachronic or sequential. The simultaneity of the four senses as used by the grammarian constitutes the resonance of the *logos,* just as the five divisions, when used by the orator, constitute the presence of the word. This is what the linguists now call *la langue,* and what Eliot calls "the auditory imagination." The auditory imagination includes both the four senses and the five divisions:

> What I call the "auditory imagination" is the feeling for syllable and rhythm, penetrating far below the conscious levels of thought and feeling, invigorating every word; sinking to the most primitive

and forgotten, returning to the origin and bringing something back, seeking the beginning and the end. It works through meanings, certainly, or not without meanings in the ordinary sense, and fuses the old and obliterated and the trite, the current, and the new and surprising, the most ancient and the most civilized mentality.[61]

Unlike the sequential parts of a speech, the five divisions are, in fact, nothing else than the five mental faculties of man, perceived comprehensively. The *logos*, especially as understood by the pre-Socratics, includes them all, but rhetoric and later philosophy alike tended to fragment and specialize the *logos* (which was translated from Greek as *ratio et oratio*). Both the ideal poet and the ideal orator shared the encyclopedic training indispensable to true eloquence.

Here are the five divisions as they appear in the work of Cicero:

> And, since all the activity and ability of an orator falls into five divisions, I learned that he must first hit upon what to say; then manage and marshal his discoveries, not merely in orderly fashion, but with a discriminating eye for the exact weight as it were of each argument; next go on to array them in the adornments of style; after that keep them guarded in his memory; and in the end deliver them with effect and charm....[62]

The poets of preliteracy hold the key to tropology and to the moral and anagogical levels: *mimesis*. De Lubac is quite explicit about the process, though he does not use the word *mimesis* when he discusses the mystical *experience* of the last two senses of Scripture.

First, the "trope" in "tropology" is a turning-inward. History and allegory are *out there*, outwardly manifested and available to the outward senses. So, after two levels of outward attention, comes the big trope, the process of interiorization:

> Now... It is no longer we who are acting; it is these words, once having been introduced, which act within us, releasing the spirit of which they have been made, the meaning and sonority included within them, and which veritably become spirit and life, and action-producing words. They belong to a place beyond our mental control; there is a certain irresistible force of authority and order in them. But they have ceased to be exterior; they have become ourselves. *And the Word was made flesh and dwelt among us*; one must understand the whole captivating, appropriating power of these two words: *in nobis*.[63]

The experience de Lubac here describes is of exactly the same pattern as the *mimesis* used by Homer and the oral-poetic establishment before the introduction of the alphabet. *Mimesis* is the technique of interiorization: knowing by putting-on, knowing by becoming, intellectually and emotionally, the thing known. That is, integral, interiorized knowing instead of conceptual knowing: unmediated, direct perception by the body and the emotions and the intellect of the hearer; in other words, by the hearer's soul. Direct experience by total submergence. De

Lubac frequently links interiorization to the moral sense (and, later, to the anagogic sense). The trope in tropology is also a turning—from symbolic theology to mystical theology.

Gilson points out that

> ...to know is to be in a new and richer way than before, since it is essentially to cause to enter into a thing which is in the first place for itself alone what another thing is in the first place for itself alone.[64] This fact is expressed by the statement that to know a thing is a kind of becoming that thing.[65]

Or, as the maxim goes, "the cognitive agent is and becomes the thing known." Proficiency with such unmediated direct perception would call for much experience of contemplation on the beholder's part. So these mystical senses of the Scriptures would be particularly available to contemplatives—the monastic orders.

Plato decided to champion the rationality that appeared in Greece alongside the phonetic alphabet. He declared war on the poets and their use of *mimesis* to communicate the oral encyclopedia.[66] *Mimesis* was the exact opposite of rational objectivity and detachment—traits that characterize the phonetic alphabet.[67] The classicist Eric Havelock pays careful attention to the matter in *Preface to Plato*:

> Plato is describing a total technology of the preserved word... a state of total personal involvement and therefore of emotional identification with the substance of the poetized statement... A modern student thinks he does well if he diverts a tiny

fraction of his psychic powers to memorize a single sonnet of Shakespeare. He is not more lazy than his Greek counterpart. He simply pours his energy into book-reading and learning through the use of his eyes instead of his ears. His Greek counterpart had to mobilize the psychic resources necessary to memorize Homer and the poets... To identify with the performance as an actor does with his lines was the only way it could be done. You threw yourself into the situation of Achilles, you identified with his grief or his anger. You yourself became Achilles and so did the reciter to whom you listened. Thirty years later you could automatically quote what Achilles had said or what the poet had said about him. Such enormous powers of poetic memorization could be purchased only at the cost of total loss of objectivity... This then is the master clue to Plato's choice of the word *mimesis* to describe the poetic experience. It focuses initially not on the artist's creative act but on his power to make his audience identify almost pathologically and certainly sympathetically with the content if what he is saying... what [Plato] is saying is that any poetized statement must be designed and recited in such a way as to make it a kind of drama within the soul both of the reciter and hence also of the audience. This kind of drama, this way of reliving experience in memory instead of analyzing and understanding it, is for him the "enemy."[68]

Havelock points out that:

> Plato was correctly concerned with the emotional pathology of the poetic performance, and it explains also why he chose the term *mimesis* to describe several aspects of the poetic experience which we today feel should be distinguished. The translation "imitation," it can now be seen, does not adequately translate his word. "Imitation" in English presumes a separate existence of an original which is then copied. The essence of Plato's point, the *point* of his attack, is that in poetic performance as practiced until then in Greece there was no "original."[69]

He says later in the book:

> The minstrel recited the tradition, and the audience listened, repeated, and recalled and so absorbed it. But the minstrel recited effectively only as he re-enacted the doings and sayings of heroes and made them his own, a process which can be described in reverse as making himself "resemble" them in endless succession. He sank his personality into his performance. His audience in turn would remember only as they entered effectively and sympathetically into what he was saying and this in turn meant that they became his servants and submitted to his spell. As they did this, they engaged also in a re-enactment of the tradition with lips, larynx, and limbs, and with the whole apparatus of their unconscious nervous system. The pattern of behavior of artist and

audience was therefore in some important respects identical. It can be described mechanically as a continual repeating of rhythmic doings. Psychologically, it is an act of personal commitment, of total engagement and of emotional identification.[70]

The "pattern of behaviour" brought into play by the poets is the same experience described by de Lubac above as tropological knowing. Tropology entails using all of the senses, of both modes of *sensus communis*, simultaneously.

Havelock's observation that the modern student "simply pours his energy into book-reading and learning through the use of his eyes instead of his ears" echoes strangely two familiar statements by St. Paul. "Faith comes by hearing..." he wrote to the Romans (10:17); that is, it would appear now, faith comes by *mimesis*, by participatory experience, not as mere concepts.[71] This saying has long seemed mysterious and enigmatic to us, but considered in the context of a society of non-literates still susceptible to the mimetic spell it would be an accurate technical observation about the operation of media. The second statement is another familiar, and puzzling, declaration: "The letter killeth but the spirit giveth life" (2 Corinthians 3:6). This, too, could be read as a technical observation about the effect of alphabetic writing: it kills *mimesis*, as Plato knew, and Aristotle, too. Both men were at pains to sidestep *mimesis* and the spellbinding power of the poetic establishment that relied on it, in order to take advantage of detachment and abstract thought— the *logos hendiathetos*.[72] Plato's war on the poets, as recapitulated by Havelock in *Preface to Plato*, was thus the first all-out media war. For at stake was nothing less than the entire enterprise of abstract thought and the new mode of philosophy. Aristotle, for his part, found that the habit of thinking in images and emotions was a major impediment to the sensibility that he required of his students, and he took steps to evade that pernicious habit. Perhaps the major tool in his counteroffensive against the lingering poetic sensibility was the syllogism: it is impossible to syllogize in images.[73] It just can not be done. (See more on this in Appendix One, "Aristotle's Media War," *infra*.)

Notes

3   "By grace you are saved through faith, and that not of yourselves, for it is the gift of God" (Eph. 2:8–9).
4   St. Thomas Aquinas, *Summa Theologica*. vol. 3, II–II, QQ 1–148. Q. 6, Art. 1, *Respondeo*.
5   Michael Waldstein, "Introduction" to *Man and Woman He Created Them: A Theology of the Body*, by Pope John Paul II (Boston: Pauline Books & Media, 2006), p. 82.
6   The included quotation is from John Paul II, *Sources of Renewal: The Implementation of the Second Vatican Council* (San Francisco: Harper & Row, 1980), pp. 203–204.
7   John Paul II, in his inaugural encyclical, *Redemptor Hominis* (Rome: Libreria Editrice Vaticana, 1979), p. 7.
8   Henri de Lubac, *Medieval Exegesis: The Four Senses of Scripture*, in four vols: vol. II. Tr. E. M. Macierowski (Grand Rapids, MI: William B. Eerdmans; Edinburgh, Scotland: T&T Clark, 2000), p. 108. Each of the quoted phrases carries extensive footnotes, all of which I have omitted here.
9   "...*quid allegoria nisi mystica mysteriorum doctrina?*": Peter Damian, *In Jud.*, c. Iv (Migne, *Patrologia Latina*, CXLV, 1082 D), *Patrologia Latina*, hereinafter referred-to as PL.
10 Richard, *Nonn. Alleg.* (PL, CXCVI, 200 BC). Cf. Nicholas of Lyra: "If the things signified by the words are referred to signify those that are to be believed in the new law, in this way

the allegorical sense is at stake."—"*Si res significatae per voces referantur ad significandum ea quae sunt in nova lege credenda, sic accipitur sensus allegoricus*" (CXIII, 28 D).

11 Joachim of Flora, *Sup. 4 ev*: "Hence, since the event was congruous with Scripture and the word that Jesus had preached, they believed the one on the basis of the other"—"*Quia ergo res gesta conveniens fuit cum Scriptura et sermone quem praedixerit Jesus, crediderunt alterum per alterum etc.*" (Buonaiuti, 247).

12 de Lubac, *op. cit.*, pp. 112–13.

13 Rhetoric distinguished two kinds of figures of speech: schemes (variations of word order for effect) and tropes (turns of phrase). The tropes included metaphor, irony, synecdoche, metonymy, alliteration, paranomasia (puns), simile, analogy, zeugma, oxymoron, paradox, hyperbole, litotes, erotema, aporia, prosopopoeia, and dozens upon dozens of others. See compendia such as Peacham's *The Garden of Eloquence* (1577), or George Puttenham's *The Arte of English Poesie* (also sixteenth century), or, for a more recent entry, Richard Lanham's *A Handlist of Rhetorical Terms* (Berkeley/Los Angeles/Oxford: University of California Press, 2nd ed., 1991).

14 de Lubac, II, p. 129.

15 Greek, *gramma*, in Latin, *littera*; hence, "grammar," meaning "literature." A grammarian is a man of letters. The letters are properly not a sense of Scripture but a technology, a medium (apart from the *sensus communis*) of translating one bodily sense into another, from ear to eye, and they exist as technological facts in the same manner that the ink and the papyrus or vellum or paper and the codex or the book are technologies. A small confusion is always present

when littera or literal is used to refer to the narrative that is written down: littera/literal is a metonymy for the narrative content of the writing on the page. In its turn, "history" (from Greek, ἰστορία) does refer to something specific, that is, the new writing style introduced by the phonetic alphabet with its emphasis on sequentiality; at the time, prose narrative was displacing poetized statement. So "historical sense" is a far less ambiguous and more appropriate term than "literal sense."

16 The "mysticus moralitatis sensus": Godfrey of Admont, h. 30, *in annunt*. 4: "*Quidquid enim legimus vel intelligimus, totum ad interioris hominis usum conferre poterimus. Si ergo totum veteris ac novi Testamenti seriem enucleatius perscrutari velimus, mysticum moralitatis sensum inditum ubique invenimus*" (PL, CLXXIV, 765 B).

17 de Lubac, II, p. 132.

18 Bernard, in *Cant.*, s. 22, n. 2: "*In hujusmodi non capit intelligentia, nisi quantum experiential attingit*" (PL, CLXXXIII, 976 C).

19. S. on *Emmäus*, n. 20: "*Incipiens a Moyse etc. Beati qui noverunt gustu felicis experientiae, quam dulciter, quam mirabiliter in oratione et meditatione Scripturas dignatur Dominus revelare*" (PL, CLXXXIV, 976 C); n. 34 (979–80). Aelred, S. *Ined.*, 4: "*Legite, quaeso, in libro experientiae*" (Talbot, p. 49, following Bernard).

20. de Lubac, II, p. 174.

21. *Ibid.*, p. 187.

22. *Ibid.*, p. 194.

23. That is, unmediated, directly perceived, experienced.

24. de Lubac, *ibid.*, p. 196. The original: ...*Mens humana, certae contemplationis gradibus ad summa conscendens, sacra*

divini eloquii inspection caelestia secreta etiam anagogice contemplator; et si ex duobus generibus visionum ad omnem perfectionem ascendit, quae per gratiam divinae revelationis theologorum et prophetarum mentibus fuit infusa; quod (primum) genusvisionis graece theophanias, id est, divinas apparitions appellabant; alterumm quo ascensu mentis et excess nude et pure et absqueintegumento, sicut est, illum caelestem sacratissimum nititur contemplari quod anagogicum nuncupatur.

Sed in hoc ultimo genere visionis ita tremuit et palpitate mens humana, ut tenebris ignorantiae suae obvoluta, ad illam claritatem et veritatis lumen, nisi dirigatur, exire nonpotest; sed quasi caeca et manductione utens, quo non videt incedit; et incipit liquefieri per visionem etvisitationem Dilecti; ut nec illud de Deo comncipiat, cum caelestis regni circumvelatum ultra, et divini luminis incircumscriptum adhuc investigare nititur, et deficit investigans. Haeret in contemplation mens attonita, obstupescit trepida, loquens penitus obmutescit, et inopem reddit copia, quam fecerat inopia copiosam; miroque modo proficiendo deficit, et tunc magis proficit, cum venerit ad defectum... s. 23 (PL, CCV, 730 AB).

25. Ibid., p. 197.
26. de Lubac's note: Cf. Rabanus, in Ruth, c. xiii: *"Corrigia ergo calceamente est ligature mysterii, Joannes itaque solver corrigiam calceamente ejus non valet, quia incarnationis ejus mysterium nec ipse investigare sufficit, qui hanc per prophetiae spiritum agnovit"* (PL, CVIII 1218 D).
27. de Lubac, ibid., p. 204.
28. Aristotle held that "the particular senses are all developments of touch, depending on the intervention of a more refined medium. Taste, for instance, apprehends the savory properties of bodies through the intermediary of moisture;

smell, the odorous conveyed through the air... Besides the specific senses there is the *sensus communis*, which is not a sixth sense but a generic power of sensation as such which provides unity for the sensitive soul in its particular manifestations. The ear does not see; however, the man who hears also sees, and some qualities are presented through more than one sense—for example roundness by sight and touch... We also perceive that we perceive through *sensus communis*." *The Encyclopedia of Philosophy*, Ed. Paul Edwards. New York: Collier Macmillan, 1967, rpt. 1972. Vol. 7, p. 3.

29. *Ad primum ergo dicendum quod sensus interior non dicitur communis per praedicationem, sicut genus; sed sicut communis radix et principium exteriorum sensus. S.T.*, Q. 78, A.4, reply to Obj. 1.

30. *S.T.*, Q. 78, A. 4, Reply to Obj. 2. See also Q. 57, Art. 2, *Respondeo*: "...thus in man himself it is manifest that the common sense which is higher than the proper sense, although it is but one faculty, knows everything apprehended by the five outward senses, and some things which no outer sense knows; for example the difference between white and sweet."

31. E.g., "It is postulated that just as white is a result of the assembling of the primary colours in ratio, so touch is an assembly of all the senses in ratio. Black is, therefore, the after-image of touch." Marshall McLuhan and Harley Parker, *Through the Vanishing Point: Space in Poetry and Painting* (New York: Harper and Row, 1968), p. 15.

32. Gilson's note, p. 475: "*Hujusmodi autem viventia inferior, quorum actus est anima, de qua nunc agitur, habent duplex esse. Unum quidem material, in quo convenient cum aliis rebus materialibus. Aliud autem immateriale, in quo communicant cum*

substantiis superioribus aliqualiter." In *II de Anima*, 5; ed. Pirotta, n. 282.
33. *The Christian Philosophy of St. Thomas Aquinas*, p. 225.
34. A fact that Nominalism denies, insisting that words are abstract, arbitrary labels. See below, p. 40, note 76.
35. de Lubac, II, pp. 203–205.
36. *S.T.*, Q. 76, Art. 1, *Sed Contra*. I.e., the intellectual principle is the formal cause of man's humanity.
37. *Ibid.*, *Respondeo*.
38. "origo fundamentum et liberalium atrium": Quntilian, followed by Isidore, Etym., 1. 1, c. 5, n. 1 (PL, LXXXII, 81 BC). William of Conches, *De philosophia mundi*: "Since grammar goes first in every teaching"—"*Quoniam in omni doctrina grammatical praecedit*" (Thurot, 17). Rabanus, Cl. Inst., 1. 3, c. 18 (CVII, 395–6). Dante, Paradiso, 12, 138: "*La prima arte.*" On Grammar in the Middle Ages: Heinrich Roos, SJ, *Die Modi significandi des Martinus de Dacia* (1952), pp. 84–99.
39. "*instrument de recherché intellectuelle*": Fontaine, pp. 29–30, analysing in Macrobius, and then Isidore "the gradual absorption of all the domains of knowledge into a single grammatical erudition with unbounded ambitions"—"l'absorption graduelle des tous les domains du savoir dans une érudition grammaticale aux ambitions démesurées." El. Elorduy, "S. Isidoro, unidad orgánica de su educación reflejada en sus escritos, la gramática ciencia totalitaria" (*Misc. Isidor.*, 1936, p. 293).
40. *Capitul. De Scholis* (MGH, Cap., 1, 79). An argument of this sort seemed "singular" and "puerile" to Hauréau. Someone may ask, "Why?"
41. "*sciential recte loquendi*"; "*sciential vere loquendi*": Isidore, *loc. cit*. William of Shyreswood: "The science of speech ... has

three parts: grammar, which teaches speaking correctly; rhetoric, which teaches speaking with embellishment; and logic, which teaches speaking truly"—"*Sermocinalis scientia ... tres habet partes: grammaticam, quae docet recte loquendi; et rhetoricam, quae docet ornate loquendi; et logicam, quae docet vere loqui*" (Roos, p. 109).

42. P. Vignaux, *Philosophie au m. âge* (1958), 7: "Grammar and logic, closely kindred disciplines"—"La grammaire et la logique, disciplines assez proches l'une et l'autre"; cf. 22 John Scotus, *De div. nat.*, 1. 5, c. 4: Grammar, like Rhetoric, is a "member of dialectic" (PL CXXII, 869–70). That is again the case, despite the disdainful opposition affected by the grand prelate Adalberon of Laon in his *Carmen ad Robertum*, v. 315.
43. *Medieval Exegesis*, vol. III, p. 62.
44. The λόγος σπερματικόσ.
45. A carpenter (efficient cause) may construct a habitable building, but it does not become a house until it houses someone. The user (formal cause) makes it a house.
46. *The Christian Philosophy of St. Thomas Aquinas*, p. 187.
47. *Ibid.*
48. *Ibid.*, pp. 187–88.
49. *Ibid.*, p. 188.
50. *Ibid.*, p. 193.
51. John Paul II, *Veritatis Splendor* (London: Catholic Truth Society/Dublin: Veritatis Publications, 1993), p. 48.
52. *Man and Woman He Created Them: A Theology of the Body*, pp. 104–105. Italics are in the original.
53. *Ibid.*, p. 197.
54. Varro, *De Lingua Latina*, Books V-VII, Book V, 7–8. Loeb Classical Library. Tr. Roland G. Kent (Cambridge, MA:

Harvard University Press, 1938, 1951), p. 9. Varro himself was not being audacious in this proposal, being a thoroughgoing traditionalist and conservative. J. K. Newman relates, in *Augustus and the New Poetry* (pp. 36–37), Varro's role in advancing the renaissance that Augustus was setting into motion:

Had Augustan poets looked to Maecenas for example rather than patronage it is clear that the title "Augustan" would have signified nothing more profound than a date. Their poetry would have been a continuation of that extraordinary movement which had begun in the earlier part of the century... and which, in spite of the grumbles of renegades like Cicero, who had begun his poetical career as a member of the new school by translating Aratus, was to prove the most constant element, the ground-bass from which all melodies were to take their key, in the work of Roman poets right up to the very end, when Rome's last great secular poet, Claudian, actually came from Alexandria itself.

But this Alexandrian influence was to be found not simply in Maecenas's actual poetry. It was built into the system of state patronage of the arts, established by Augustus and modelled directly on a scheme propounded by Julius. What Julius had done was to commission Varro to gather as many Greek and Latin works as he could into a library, which was then to become a centre of studies with the indefatigable Varro himself at its head. In the context of the times there can only have been one precedent for this action, and that was the establishment by the Hellenistic monarchs in their cities of similar centres of learning. The first and most important of these was of course the Library and Museum of Alexandria. Scholars disagree whether the Palatine Library and Temple of Apollo subsequently opened by Augustus in 28 was the successor to this scheme of Julius, or whether it was an independent foundation made after Asinius Pollo had completed Julius's original project, but the main idea seems clear. Just as in Alexandria, so in Rome poetry and the arts were to be under the special protection of the court and government, and would find that the only road to success lay in easy relations with the established authorities.

The influence which this library had on Augustan poetry is not perhaps always sufficiently stressed. For example, Rostagni states quite rightly: "The greatest Augustan poets were actually formed directly in the school of the *poetae novi* and also in a certain sense of Lucretius. They continued the direction... of the so-called 'new poetry'..." but he confines his remarks about the Library to a few lines. What Augustus was doing here... was to unite two traditions: an older one, in which... a guild of *scribae et histriones* had met at the temple of Minerva and had there enjoyed the official state recognition and tolerance accorded to other collegia by Roman law; and a younger one, modelled more directly on Hellenistic practice, in which... the *scribae et histriones* of the new age (the poets among the *scribae* with a new name) were to be encouraged to contribute more actively to the common good.

55 Psalm 113:1–2 (114:1–2 in the King James Version).
56 *Literary Criticism of Dante Alighieri*, tr. And ed. Robert S. Haller (Lincoln, NB: University of Nebraska Press, 1973), p. 99.
57 This usage is most clearly evident when the reader notices that the fifth movement of each poem concerns words and expression. Eliot was not alone in this regard. Other poets of his time had used the five divisions extensively in their

poetry, poets such as Wordsworth, Shelley, Ezra Pound, W. B. Yeats, Wyndham Lewis.
58 The motto of Mary, Queen of Scots.
59 Quintilian, *Institutio Oratoria*, Loeb Classical Library, Book I, iv.1–4. Tr. H. E. Butler (Cambridge, MA; London: William Heinemann, 1963), I, 63.
60 *Ibid*. Book III, iii, 1–3, I, 385.
61 T. S. Eliot, *The Use of Poetry & the Use of Criticism: Studies in the Relation of Criticism to Poetry in England* (London: Faber and Faber, 1933), pp. 118–19.
62 *De Oratore*, in two vols., tr. E. W. Sutton, vol. I (Cambridge, MA Loeb Classical Library, 1942; rpt. 1967), XXXI, pp. 99, 98.
63 de Lubac, II, p. 140.
64 In Thomistic language, since a being is defined by its form, a knowing being is distinguished from a nonknowing one in that it possesses, besides its own proper form, the form of the thing it knows: "*Cognoscentia a non cognoscentibus in hoc distinguuntur, quia non cognoscentia nihil habent, nisi formam suum tantum, sed cognoscens natum est habere formam etiam rei alterius; nam species cogniti est in cognoscente. Unde manifestum est, quod natura rei non cognoscentis est magis coarctata et limita. Natura autem rerum cognoscentium habet majorem amplitudinem et extenssionem; propter quod dicit Philosophus, III De Anima* (text 37) *quod anima est quodammodo omnia.*" *S.T.*, I, 14, [Gilson's note]
65 Gilson, *The Christian Philosophy of St. Thomas Aquinas*, p. 224. (See also pp. 226–27.) He notes (p. 474, n. 2): In Thomistic language, since a being is defined by its form, a knowing being is distinguished from a nonknowing one in that it possesses, besides its own proper form, the form of the thing it knows: "*Cognoscentia a non cognoscentibus*

in hoc distinguuntur, quia non cognoscentia nihil habent, nisi formam suum tantum, sed cognoscens natum est habere formam etiam rei alterius; nam species cogniti est in cognoscente. Unde manifestum est, quod natura rei non cognoscentis est magis coarctata et limita. Natura autem rerum cognoscentium habet majorem amplitudinem et extensionem; propter quod dicit Philosophus, III De Anima (text. 37) *quod anima est quodammodo omnia."* S.T., I, 14, 1. Such, too, is the meaning of the well-known statement of John of St. Thomas: *"Cognoscentia autem in hoc elevantur super non cognoscentia, quia id quod alterius, ut alterius, seu prout manet distinctum in alteropossunt in se recipere, ita quod in se sunt, sed etiam possunt fieri alia a se." De Anima,* IV, 1. This statement is not St. Thomas's, but it is consistent with his thinking.

66 The εγκύκλιος παιδεια.

67 I have discussed this matter in detail in *Laws of Media: The New Science* (Toronto, ON: University of Toronto Press, 1988).

68 Havelock, Eric, *Preface to Plato* (Cambridge, MA: Harvard University Press, 1963), pp. 44–45.

69 *Op. cit.*, p. 159. See, for explication, Havelock's lengthy footnote no. 22 to chapter 3, covering pp. 57–60.

70 *Op. cit.*, pp. 159–60.

71 Cf. "Hence, if we want to understand what faith is, we need to follow the route it has taken, the path trodden by believers, as witnessed first in the Old Testament. Here a unique place belongs to Abraham, our father in faith. Something disturbing takes place in his life: God speaks to him; he reveals himself as a God who speaks and calls his name. Faith is linked to hearing. Abraham does not see God, but he hears his voice. Faith thus takes on a personal aspect." Pope

Francis, *The Light of Faith* (*Lumen Fidei*) (Libreria Editrice Vaticana / San Francisco: Ignatius Press, 2013), p. 17.

72 λόγος ἐνδιάθετοσ.

73 See Appendix One, *infra*.

SYNESTHESIA

ABOUT TEN PEOPLE IN a million live extraordinarily rich sensory lives. They live, that is, in full conscious awareness of the *sensus communis*: they live every moment of their lives submerged in the interactions of each of the senses with all of the others: they are called synesthetes. Writes Dr. Richard Cytowic:

> Imagine that you are a synesthete, like Michael Watson. You are standing in front of the refrigerator late at night trying to decide on a snack. You look at the leftover roast but you say to yourself, "No, I'm not in the mood for arches." Or, contemplating a slice of lemon meringue pie, decide you aren't hungry for points. You dismiss the thought of a peanut butter sandwich because you know you couldn't sleep well if you stuffed yourself full of spheres and circles.
>
> There you stand, bathed in the refrigerator light, casting your eye from shelf to shelf. You shift your feet against the cool floor and finally take a slice of chocolate mint pie. As you do, you feel a dozen

columns before you, invisible to the eye but real to the touch. You set the fork down and run your hand up and down their cool, smooth surfaces. As you roll the minty taste in your mouth your outstretched hand rubs the back curve of one of the columns. What a sumptuous sensation. The surface feels cool, refreshing, even sexual in a way."[74]

Early in his researches, Dr. Cytowic came across *The Mind of a Mnemonist*, A. R. Luria's account of his patient known simply as "S." "S was not aware of any distinct line separating vision from hearing, or hearing from any other sense. He could not suppress the translation of sounds into taste, shape, touch, colour, and movement."

Presented with a tone pitched at 2,000 cycles per second, "S" said, "it looks something like fireworks tinged with a pink-red hue. The strip of colour feels rough and unpleasant, and it has an ugly taste— rather like a briny pickle... you could hurt your hand on this."

The same synesthesia enabled him to visualize vividly each word or sound that he heard, whether in his own tongue or in a language unintelligible to himself. The thing to be remembered automatically *converted itself* without effort on his part into a visual image of such durability that he could remember it years after the initial encounter. So specific was his ability that the same stimuli would produce the exact synesthetic response.

> "S" was a person who "saw" everything, who had to feel a telephone number on the tip of his tongue before he could remember it. He could not understand anything unless an impression of it leaked through all his senses.[75]

On display here is the bodily *sensus communis* in full operation. Here is how S described his world:

> I recognize a word not only by the images it evokes, but by a whole complex of feelings that image arouses... it's not a matter of vision or hearing but some over-all sense I get. Usually, I experience a word's taste and weight, and I don't have to make an effort to remember it— the word seems to recall itself. But it's difficult to describe. What I sense is something oily slipping through my hand... or I'm aware of a slight tickling in my left hand caused by a mass of tiny, light-weight points. When this happens, I simply remember, without having to make the attempt.[76]

S's experience of words, reported in various ways by all other synesthetes, brings immediately to mind Grammar's insistence on Realism (rather than Nominalism) as the *raison d'être* for etymology as a science, the observation that words are rooted in experience, that words are the storehouse of experience, and that words have a real relation to the things and processes they name.[77] And that a language is an organ of perception.

Like S, a synesthete simply experiences his *sensus communis* in the foreground of his awareness while the rest of us have it operating behind the scenes, outside consciousness.[78] The mystical experience of anagogy, too, relies on the *sensus communis* both of body and of intellect. There is no place in anagogy for detachment or objectivity.

Concerning objectivity, there is the testimony of Jacques Lusseyran, who, when he was seven years old, was blinded in a schoolyard mishap. He recovered vision almost instantly through the operation of the *sensus communis*:

> I did not become a musician, and the reason was a strange one. I had no sooner made a sound on the A string, on D or G or C, than I no longer heard it. I looked at it. Tones, chords, melodies, rhythms, each was immediately transformed into pictures, curves, lines, shapes, landscapes, and most of all colours. Whenever I made the A string sound by itself with the bow, such a burst of light appeared before my eyes and lasted so long that often I had to stop playing.
>
> At concerts, for me, the orchestra was like a painter. It flooded me with all the colours of the rainbow. If the violin came in by itself, I was suddenly filled with gold and fire, and with red so bright I could not remember having seen it on any object. When it was the oboe's turn, a clear green ran all through me, so cool that I seemed to feel the breath of night. I visited the land of music. I rested my eyes on every one of its scenes. I loved it till it caught my breath. But I saw music too much to be

able to speak its language. My own language was the language of shapes.

Strange chemistry, the chemistry which changed a symphony into a moral purpose, an adagio into a poem, a concerto into a walk, attaching words to pictures and pictures to words, daubing the world with colours and finally making the human voice into the most beautiful of all instruments![79]

He goes on:

> For my part I had an idea of people, an image, but not the one seen by the world at large. Frankly, hair, eyes, mouth, the necktie, the rings on fingers mattered very little to me. I no longer even thought about them. People no longer seemed to possess them. Sometimes in my mind men and women appeared without heads or fingers. Then again, the lady in the chair rose before me in her bracelet, turned into the bracelet itself. There were people whose teeth seemed to fill their whole faces, and others so harmonious they seemed to be made of music. But in reality none of these sights is made to be described. They are so mobile, so much alive that they defy words.
>
> People were not at all as they were said to be and never the same for more than two minutes at a stretch. Some were, of course, but that was a bad sign, a sign that they did not want to understand or be alive, that they were somehow caught in the glue of some indecent passion. That kind of thing

I could see in them right away, because, not having their faces before my eyes, I caught them off guard. People are not accustomed to this, for they only dress up for those who are looking at them.[80]

Moreover, he finds that he can read voices like a book.

What voices taught me they taught me almost at once. I ended by reading so many things into voices without wanting to, without even thinking about it, that voices concerned me more than the words they spoke. Sometimes, for minutes at a time in class, I heard nothing, neither the teacher's questions nor the answers of my comrades. I was too much absorbed in the images their voices were parading through my head. All the more since these images half the time contradicted, and flagrantly, the appearance of things...

A beautiful voice (and beautiful means a great deal in this context, for it means that the man who has such a voice is beautiful himself) remains so through coughing and stammering. An ugly voice, on the contrary, can become soft, scented, humming, singing like the flute. But to no purpose. It stayed ugly just the same... as for hypocrites, they were recognizable immediately.[81]

Lusseyran characterizes his synesthetic sense as a sort of limitless mental screen:

Names, figures, and objects in general did not

> appear on my screen without shape, not just in black and white, but in all the colours of the rainbow. Still, I never remember consciously encouraging this phenomenon. Nothing entered my mind without being bathed in a certain amount of light. To be more precise, everything from living creatures to ideas appeared to be carved out of the primordial light. In a few months, my personal world had turned into a painter's studio.
>
> I was not the master of these apparitions. The number five was always black, the letter L light green, and kindly feeling a soft blue. There was nothing I could do about it, and when I tried to change the colour of a sign, the sign at once clouded over and at once disappeared. A strange power, imagination! It certainly functioned in me but also in spite of me.[82]

More pertinent to our investigation, perhaps, is his observation about the effect of tinkering with the senses. For half a century now, it has been a commonplace of media studies that each technology extends one or another sense or faculty, according it a sort of hyperesthesia, which has then the effect of numbing the bodily sense extended and rearranging the interplay between the other senses—what we have been calling the *sensus communis*.[83]

> When I came across the myth of objectivity in certain modern thinkers, it made me angry. So there was only one world for these people, the same for everyone. And all the other worlds were to be

counted as illusions left over from the past. Or why not call them by their name— hallucinations? I had learned to my cost how wrong they were.

From my own experience I knew very well that it was enough to take from a man a memory here, an association there, to deprive him of hearing or sight, for the world to undergo immediate transformation, and for another world, entirely different but entirely coherent, to be born. Another world? Not really. The same world rather, but seen from another angle, and counted in entirely new measures. When this happened, all the hierarchies they called objective were turned upside down, scattered to the four winds, not even like theories but like whims.

The psychologists more than all the rest—there were a few exceptions, Bergson among them— seemed to me not to come within miles of the heart of the matter, the inner life. They took it as their subject but did not talk about it. They were as embarrassed in its presence as a hen finding out that she has hatched a duckling. Of course, I was more uneasy than they were when it came to talking about it, but not when it came to living it. I was only sixteen years old, and I felt it was up to them to tell me. Yet they told me nothing.[84]

Fortunately, Lusseyran has set down a remarkably detailed account of his recovery of sight. It is not optical vision, as you and I know it, but sight as registered by the other senses in the *sensus communis*:

It was a great surprise to me to find myself blind, and being blind was not at all as I imagined it. Nor was it as the people around me seemed to think it. They told me that to be blind meant not to see. Yet how was I to believe them when I saw? Not at once, I admit. Not in the days immediately after the operation. For at that time I still wanted to use my eyes. I followed their usual path. I looked in the direction where I was in the habit of seeing before the accident, and there was anguish, a lack, something like a void which filled me with what grownups called despair.

Finally, one day, and it was not long in coming, I realized that I was looking in the wrong way. It was as simple as that. I was making something very like the mistake people make who change their glasses without adjusting themselves. I was looking too far off, and too much on the surface of things...

At this point some instinct—I was almost about to say a hand laid on me—made me change course. I began to look more closely, not at things but at a world closer to myself, looking from an inner place to one further within,[85] instead of clinging to the movement of sight toward the world outside.

Immediately, the substance of the universe drew together, redefined and peopled itself anew. I was aware of a radiance emanating from a place I knew nothing about, a place which might as well have been outside me as within. But radiance was there, or, to put it more precisely, light. It was a fact, for light was there.

I felt indescribable relief, and happiness so great it almost made me laugh. confidence and gratitude came as if a prayer had been answered. I found light and joy at the same moment, and I can say without hesitation that from that time on light and joy have never been separated in my experience. I have had them or lost them together...[86]

I am quoting Lusseyran's history at length because of his unique ability to display for us the common sense in operation. His account is the more useful in that he does not once refer to a common sense: he is unaware that there is any such thing. There is no theory here; everything he relates is actual experience, experience actually available to anyone.[87] His blindness aside, Lusseyran was in all respects an ordinary human being. The *sensus communis* he describes is that of the physical body. It is not hallucination but normal experience, extraordinary only in being observed and related. His account has obvious similarities to reports of the mystical experience of anagogy, but they are not at all the same thing; the anagogical experience is a compound of both modes of sense, inner and outer, sacred and bodily, the Book of Scripture and the Book of Nature. My intention in these lines is not to explain away anagogy or the mystical experience; rather, I hope to shed some light on the processes involved and to indicate something of their relation to human faculties and human perception, mediated and unmediated.

Toward that end, let us catch a little more of Lusseyran's remarkable account:

> The amazing thing was that this was not magic for me at all, but reality. I could no more have denied it

than people with eyes can deny that they see. I was not light myself, I knew that, but I bathed in it as an element which blindness had brought much closer. I could feel light rising, spreading, resting on objects, giving them form, then leaving them. Withdrawing or diminishing is what I mean, for the opposite of light was never present. Sighted people always talk about the night of blindness, and that seems to them quite natural. But there is no such night, for at every waking hour and even in my dreams I lived in a stream of light.

Without my eyes light was much more stable than it had been with them. As I remember it, there were no longer the same differences between things lighted brightly, less brightly or not at all. I saw the whole world in light, existing through it and because of it.

Colours, all the colours of the rainbow, also survived. For me, the child who loved to draw and paint, colours made a celebration so unexpected that I spent hours playing with them, and all the more easily now they were more docile than they used to be.

Light threw its colour on things and on people. My father and mother, the people I met or ran into in the street, all had their characteristic colour which I had never seen before I went blind. Yet now this special attribute impressed itself on me as part of them as definitely as any impression created by a face. Still, the colours were only a game, while light was my whole reason for living. I let it rise in me like water in a well, and I rejoiced.[88]

At one point, Lusseyran decides to test it, to resist it and see what would result:

> At night in bed, when I was all by myself, I shut my eyes. I lowered my eyelids as I might have done when they covered my physical eyes. I told myself that behind these curtains I would no longer see light. But light was still there, and more serene than ever, looking like a lake at evening when the wind has dropped. Then I gathered up all my energy and will power and tried to stop the flow of light, as I might have tried to stop breathing.
>
> What happened was a disturbance, something like a whirlpool. But the whirlpool was still flooded with light. At all events I couldn't keep this up very long, perhaps only for two or three seconds. When this was going on I felt a sort of anguish, as though I were doing something forbidden, something against life. It was exactly as if I needed light to live—needed it as much as air. There was no way out of it. I was the prisoner of light. I was condemned to see.
>
> As I write these lines, I have just tried the experiment again, with the same result, except that with the years the original source of light has grown stronger.
>
> At eight, I came out of this experiment reassured, with the sense that I was being reborn. Since it was not I who was making the light, since it came to me from outside, it would never leave me. I was only a passageway, a vestibule for this brightness. The seeing eye was in me.[89]

He does not hesitate to ascribe a spiritual character to his interiorized knowing:

> Before I was ten years old, I knew with absolute certainty that everything in the world was a sign of something else, ready to take its place if it should fall by the way. And this continuing miracle of healing I heard expressed fully in the Lord's Prayer I repeated at night before going to sleep. I was not afraid. Some people would say I had faith, and how should I not have it in the presence of the marvel which kept renewing itself? Inside me every sound, every shape, and every scent was forever changing into light, and light itself changing into colour to make a kaleidoscope of my blindness.[90]

Pope Francis offers some apposite remarks about faith and light in his first encyclical:

> The light of faith is unique, since it is capable of illuminating *every aspect* of human existence. A light this powerful cannot come from ourselves, but from a more primordial source: in a word, it must come from God. Faith is born of an encounter with the living God, who calls us and reveals his love, a love which precedes us and upon which we can lean for security and for building our lives. Transformed by this love, we gain fresh vision, new eyes to see; we realize that it contains great promise of fulfillment and that a vision of the future opens up before us. Faith, received from God as a supernatural gift,

becomes a light for our way, guiding our journey through time.[91]

This kind of observation echoes the mystical experience of Scripture:

> As I walked along a country road bordered by trees, I could point to each one of the trees by the road, even if they were not spaced at regular intervals. I knew whether the trees were straight and tall, carrying their branches as a body carries its head, or gathered into thickets and partly covering the ground around them.
>
> This kind of exercise soon tired me out, I must admit, but it succeeded. And the fatigue did not come from the trees, from their number or shape, but from myself. To see them like this I had to hold myself in a state so far removed from old habits that I could not keep it up for very long. I had to let the trees come toward me, and not allow the slightest inclination to move toward them, the smallest wish to know them, to come between them and me. I could not afford to be curious or impatient or proud of my accomplishment.[92]

(For "trees" in the last two sentences, read "Scriptures.") And here he describes unmistakably the role and the experience of *mimesis*:

> As with the sense of touch, what came to me from objects was pressure, but pressure of a kind so new

to me that at first I didn't think of calling it be that name. When I became really attentive and did not oppose my own pressure to my surroundings, the trees and rocks came to me and printed their shape upon me like fingers leaving their impression in wax.[93]

Dr. Cytowic reports, almost as an afterthought, "perhaps the strangest example of synesthesia I uncovered was 'audiomotor,' in which a fourteen-year-old boy positioned his body in different postures according to the sounds of different words"[94]:

> Both English and nonsense sounds had certain physical movements, the boy claimed, which he could demonstrate by striking various poses. By way of convincing himself that this sound-to-movement association was real, the physician who described it planned to retest the boy later on without warning. When the doctor read the same word list aloud ten years later, the boy assumed, without hesitation, the identical postures of a decade earlier.[95]

Notes

74 Richard E. Cytowic, *The Man Who Tasted Shapes: A Bizarre Medical Mystery Offers Revolutionary Insights into Emotions, Reasoning, and Consciousness* (New York: G. P. Putnam's Sons, 1993), p. 6. Numerous famous people were synesthetes, including some well-known artists. Researchers say synesthesia is eight times more common among artists than it is in the general population. A few examples: painter David Hockney, writer Vladimir Nabokov, jazz musician and composer Duke

Ellington, composer and pianist Franz Liszt, painter Vasily Kandinsky, physicist and writer Richard Feynman.

75 Cytowic, p. 33.
76 Quoted by Cytowic, *ibid*.
77 The structure of and rationale for Realism is to be found in the *sensus communis*. Of course. Nominalists insist that names are simply arbitrarily imposed on things. Realists hold that the name of a thing is its analogue, that naming entails translating the experience of the thing named, the perception (experience) of the thing, via the *sensus communis*, into another posture of the senses, another experience, that of utterance. The great example of this is found in Adam's first task in the Garden of Eden: giving names to all that he encountered. God's naming was the act of creating, of uttering all in creation. Adam's labour of naming was to process the experience of the thing being named through his pristine, pre-lapsarian *sensus communis*, to trace the path of cognition, which remained incomplete until he found (literally, "invented," from *invenire*) an appropriate name—generally the province of poets and grammarians. Finding the name completes the process of cognition and is closure for the *experience* of encountering the thing. Naming, then, constitutes a form of re-cognition. Etymology claims to be the science of retracing the labyrinth of cognition and recognition embedded in the word as far as the original experience (perception) of the thing, the *synesthetic* translation. (St. Thomas affirms more than once that every name is intended to signify the nature or the essence of something.) The word performs a re-cognition of the thing and stands in analogical ratio to the thing it names. Surely this process underlies the "objective correlative" sought by our poets a century ago.

Here is how Eliot presented the matter: "The only way of expressing emotion in the form of art is by finding an 'objective correlative'; in other words, a set of objects, a situation, a chain of events which shall be the formula of that *particular* emotion; such that when the external facts, which must terminate in sensory experience, are given, the emotion is immediately evoked." (From "Hamlet and His Problems," in *The Sacred Wood: Essays on Poetry and Criticism* [London: Methuen, 1920; New York: Barnes & Noble, 1960], p. 100). The objective correlative shares the same goal as etymology: it does not use etymology but rather consults experience directly. So the entire business calls for great delicacy of perception, and precision, and depth of learning and discernment. Hence the grammarian's insistence that a language is an organ of perception.

78 With these matters in mind, recall the power of the oral, preliterate poets against whom Plato warred. He fought against their use of *mimesis*, which also Aristotle confronted head-on.

79 Jacques Lusseyran, *And There Was Light*, tr. from the French by Elizabeth Cameron (Boston and Toronto: Little, Brown and Company, 1963), pp. 94–95.

80 *Ibid.*, p. 73.

81 *Ibid.*, pp. 76–77.

82 *Ibid.*, p. 43.

83 See Marshall McLuhan, *Understanding Media: The Extensions of Man* (New York: McGraw-Hill, 1964), and *The Gutenberg Galaxy: The Making of Typographic Man* (Toronto: University of Toronto Press, 1962).

84 *And There Was Light, op. cit.*, pp. 143–44.

85 A tropology.

86 *Ibid.*, pp. 15–17.
87 For an account of an experiment to test this assertion, see Appendix Six, *infra*.
88 *Ibid.*, pp. 17–18. Gilson, then, errs in his reasoning on this matter by not taking into account the *sensus communis*: "When a sense is lacking, all the knowledge which that sense apprehends vanishes with it. Where a sense is lacking so too is a science. Men born blind know nothing of colours. But they would know them if the intellect possessed naturally innate, intelligible motions of all things. We can go beyond mere observation of this fact, however, and show that such knowledge would not be in accord with the human soul." *The Christian Philosophy of St. Thomas Aquinas, op. cit.*, p. 213.
89 *Ibid.*, pp. 18–19.
90 *Ibid.*, p. 29.
91 *The Light of Faith, op. cit.*, p. 11.
92 *And There Was Light, op. cit.*, p. 32.
93 *Ibid.*, pp. 32–33.
94 G. Deveraux. "An Unusual Audio-Motor Synesthesia in an Adolescent," *Psychiatric Quarterly* 40(3), 1966: 459–71.
95 Cytowic, *op. cit.*, pp. 53–54

BECOMING DISCARNATE

SIMILAR TO DR. CYTOWIC'S example, just quoted, medical staff in maternity wards around the world can confirm that newborn children mime the sound of the human voice with minute twitches and muscle spasms for hours and even days after birth: for a brief time, their whole skin appears to function as a sort of eardrum. The neonate puts on the human voice with the skin, the organ of touch, the common sense of the body. We all are born, it would seem, with overt *mimesis* and synesthesia.

In recent decades, however, the neonate experience has manifested among teenagers and adults, so many of whom now prefer to play recordings extremely loud on their sound systems and their headsets, so loud that the consequent damage caused to hearing is causing widespread concern. You can hear a closed car coming down the street from a block away as the sounds (particularly the boosted bass frequencies) of the radio inside boom their massage: ironically, because of noise-restriction laws, the engine sounds must be thoroughly muffled. No longer is modern music something to listen to; it has become something to be felt, experienced with all of the senses. In movie theaters, too, the sound is so loud that it is felt in the gut;

the entire body acts as the eardrum and the ear itself drowns in sound, setting aside all capacity to discriminate subtleties in music. Furthermore, if you observe closely the average person watching a television program, you can discern the "neonate effect" of micro-movements and twitches of the face and skin in response to the images on the screen. Whole-body knowing has returned in our time in a dozen ways. *Mimesis* is whole-body knowing. These examples and others—contemporary dance modes, role-playing computer games—indicate a growing hunger for *mimesis* and everyman's preparedness to engage in it. The same propensities are reflected in the interest, increasing since the advent of television and of colour television, in the sensibilities of the Middle Ages and in the inner life—contemplation and mysticism.

In poetry, the reinstitution of *mimesis* probably began with the French Symbolists (e.g., Flaubert, Mallarmé, Baudelaire) during the nineteenth century. Baudelaire, in particular, explored synesthesia in his "correspondences." In the epigraph to the poem, he wrote candidly, "Hypocrite lecteur! Mon semblable, mon frère." The use of the term "hypocrite" is particularly meaningful; it is almost a separate poem. "Hypocrite" means mask-wearer. The reader is to wear the poem as a mask, to put it on—an act of *mimesis*—so that the poem can retune his ossified sensibilities.

The poem is designed as a corrective, a prosthetic device like eyeglasses. That this might occur, the poet first had to put on the reader's sensibilities in the act of diagnosis, another *mimesis*. T. S. Eliot refers to this complex interchange when he describes the function of meaning in a poem:

> The chief use of "meaning" of a poem, in the ordinary sense, may be (for here again I am speaking

of some kinds of poetry and not all) to satisfy one habit of the reader, to keep his mind diverted and quiet, while the poem does its work upon him: much as the imaginary burglar is always provided with a bit of nice meat for the house-dog. This is a normal situation of which I approve.[96]

Poetry and the other arts had by Eliot's time shifted their focus from serving up pleasing aesthetic objects to working directly on the *sensus communis* as a doctor works directly on the infirmities of a patient. The shift had actually begun with the Symbolists, in response to the first electric forms of communication, the telegraph and the telephone. Eliot's observation about the burglar indicates a new order of sensibility in the arts, one in which the audience is no longer allowed to be a spectator but must put on (*"Hypocrite!"*) the role of participant. So every reader will experience the poem differently as his or her sensibility conforms to the poetic situation provided by the poet.[97] It signals a shift from the conscious intellectual apprehension of words and images to the out-of-awareness bodily *sensus communis*.

It is commonplace to observe that the meaning of a poem may wholly escape paraphrase. It is not quite so commonplace to observe that the meaning of a poem may be something larger than its author's conscious purpose, and something remote from its origins. One of the more obscure of modern poets was Stéphane Mallarmé, of whom the French sometimes say that his language is so peculiar that it can be understood only by foreigners... If we are moved by a poem, it has meant something, perhaps something important, to us; if we are not moved, then it is, as poetry, meaningless. We can be deeply stirred by hearing the recitation of a poem in a language of which we understand no word; but if we are then told that the poem is gibberish and has no meaning, we shall consider that we have been deluded—this was no poem, it was merely an imitation of instrumental music. If as we are aware, only a part of the meaning can be conveyed by paraphrase, that is because the poet is occupied with frontiers of consciousness beyond which words fail, though meanings still exist. A poem may appear to mean very different things to different readers, and all of these meanings may be different from what the author thought he meant. For instance, the author may have been writing some peculiar personal experience, which he saw quite unrelated to anything outside; yet for the reader the poem may become the expression of a general situation, as well as of some private experience of his own. The reader's interpretation may differ from the author's and be equally valid—it may even be better.[98]

Sir Ernst Gombrich, in *Art and Illusion*, calls this new audience-participation "the beholder's share." In effect, the beholder becomes the accomplice of the artist, the co-creator: wherever, in the arts since the Symbolists, since Cézanne, the beholder is required to complete the work of art, there you find formal cause in operation, and there you find *mimesis*, as in the case of anagogy. We might justifiably call it not formal cause but rather *con*-formal cause. In apprehending the tropological senses of

Scripture the conforming occurs in the process of interiorization: thus de Lubac sings of the "incurable character of incompleteness" of tropology that draws the contemplative reader into its vortex.[99] This kind of conformity is also, fundamentally, a coherence. Each of the Church's sacraments, too, is a formal cause, a medium of communication, a mimetic vortex.

I spent several pages above relaying the accounts of synesthetes because their experiences with physical synesthesia and *mimesis* can assist us by analogy to understand the functioning of the mystical synesthesia in that other common sense of the soul. Certainly, the mystical experiences reported by contemplatives and many of the saints have clear echoes in the synesthetes' experiences. And while the interpretation of Scripture is generally performed one sense at a time, seriatim, as for example in Dante's illustration, master exegetes use a mosaic approach of educing all of the senses at once, synesthetically. Such is the case with John Paul II's performances in his *Male and Female He Created Them: A Theology of the* Body as, for example, in this paragraph where he sums up the significance of the resurrection:

> 4. To understand all that "the redemption of the body" implies according to Romans, an authentic theology of the body is necessary. We have attempted to build one, appealing first of all to the words of Christ. The constitutive elements of the theology of the body are contained in what Christ says when he appeals to the "beginning" concerning the question of the indissolubility of marriage (see Mt. 19:8), in what he says about concupiscence when he appeals to the human heart in the Sermon

on the Mount (see Mt. 5:28), and also in what he says when he appeals to the resurrection (see Mt. 22:30). Each one of these statements contains in itself a rich content of an anthropological as well as an ethical nature. Christ speaks to man—and speaks about man, who is a "body" and is created as male and female in the image and likeness of God; he speaks about man, whose heart is subjected to concupiscence; and, finally, about man, before whom the eschatological perspective of the resurrection of the body opens up.[100]

And again, two paragraphs later:

6. The "redemption of the body," however, expresses itself not only in the resurrection as a victory over death. It is present also in the words of Christ addressed to "historical" man, both when they confirm the principle of the indissolubility of marriage as a principle coming from the Creator himself, and when—in the Sermon on the Mount—Christ invites us to overcome concupiscence, even in the exclusively inner movements of the human heart. About both of these key statements one must say that they refer to *human morality* and have an *ethical sense*. Here it is not a question of the eschatological hope of the resurrection, but of the hope of victory over sin, which can be called the hope of everyday.[101]

The etymology, then, of the state of sinfulness is to be found in the state of original innocence; consequently, by proportional analogy, knowing (that is, perception) is to being as sin is to non-being—a statement of formal cause:

> The state of sin is part of "historical man," of the human beings about whom we read in Matthew 19, that is, of Christ's interlocutors then, as well as of every other potential or actual interlocutor at all times of history and thus, of course, of man today. Yet, in every man without exception, this state— the historical state—plunges its roots deeply into his theological "prehistory," which is the state of original innocence.[102]
>
> ...The laws of knowing correspond to those of being. It is impossible to understand the state of "historical" sinfulness without referring or appealing to the state of original (in some sense "prehistoric") and fundamental innocence (and in fact Christ appeals to it). The emergence of sinfulness as a state, as a dimension of human existence, has thus from the beginning been linked with man's real innocence as an original and fundamental state, as a dimension of being created "in the image of God." And this point applies not only to the case of the first man, male and female, as *dramatis personae* and protagonists of the events described in the Yahwist texts of Genesis 2 and 3, but also to the entire historical course of human existence. *Thus historical man is rooted, so to speak, in his revealed theological prehistory*; and for this reason, every point of his historical sinfulness must be explained (both in the case

of the soul and of the body) with reference to original innocence. One can say that this reference is a "co-inheritance" of sin, and precisely of original sin. While in every historical man this sin signifies a state of lost grace, it also carries with itself a reference to that grace, which was precisely the grace of original innocence.[103]

We must locate as exactly as possible the real *meaning* of the body before proceeding to discuss the disruptive effects of contemporary technologies of communication on our perception of the body and on the *sensus communis*.

4. In this way, we find ourselves within the very bone marrow of the anthropological reality that has the name "body." The words of Genesis 2:23 speak about this directly and for the first time in the following terms, "flesh from my flesh and bone from my bones." The man speaks these words as if it were only at the sight of the woman that he could identify and call by name *that which makes them in a visible way similar, the one to the other*, and at the same time that in which humanity is manifested. In the light of the earlier analysis of all the "bodies" man came in contact with and conceptually defined, giving them their names (*animalia*), the expression "flesh from my flesh" takes on precisely this meaning: the body reveals man. This concise formula already contains all that human science will ever be able to say about the structure of the body as an organism, about its vitality, about its particular

sexual physiology, etc. In this first expression of the man, "flesh from my flesh" contains also a reference to that by which that body is authentically human and thus to that which determines man as a person, that is, also in all its bodiliness, "similar" to God.[104]

Now we are at the crux of the matter. The body, with its *sensus communis*, and the intellectual soul, with its *sensus communis*, constitute an integral whole that is inextricably and particularly human. As John Paul II reiterates, emphatically:

> We find ourselves, therefore, within the very bone marrow of the anthropological reality whose name is "body," human body. Yet, as can easily be observed, this marrow is not only anthropological but essentially theological. The theology of the body, which is linked from the beginning with the creation of man in the image of God, becomes in some way also a theology of sex, or rather a theology of masculinity and femininity, which has its point of departure here, in Genesis. The original meaning of unity, to which the words of Genesis 2:24 bear witness was to have a broad and far-reaching perspective in God's revelation. This unity through the body ("and the two will become one flesh") possesses a multiform dimension: an ethical dimension, as is confirmed by Christ's response to the Pharisees in Matthew 19 (see also Mk. 10), and also a sacramental dimension, strictly theological, as confirmed by the words of Paul to the Ephesians,[105] that likewise refer to the tradition of the prophets

(Hosea, Isaiah, Ezekiel). And this is so because the unity that is realized through the body indicates from the beginning not only the "body," but also the "incarnate" communion of persons—*communio personarum*—and requires this communion right from the beginning. Masculinity and femininity express *the twofold aspect of man's somatic constitution* ("this time she is flesh from my flesh and bone from my bones") and *indicate*, in addition, through the same words of Genesis 2:23, *the new consciousness of the meaning of one's own body*. This meaning, one can say, consists in *reciprocal enrichment*. Precisely this consciousness, through which humanity forms itself anew as a communion of persons, seems to construe the layer in the account of the creation of man (and in the revelation of the body contained in it) that is deeper than the somatic structure as male and female. In any case, this structure is presented from the beginning with a deep consciousness of human bodiliness and sexuality, and this establishes an inalienable norm for the understanding of man on the theological plane.[106]

In the matters we have been examining in these pages, we have found that there is not one kind of *sensus communis*, but there are two: one *sensus communis* relating to the physical body, and one relating to the intellect, the soul. Accordingly, there must then be two ecologies: one of the body and corporal senses, and one of the soul and intellectual senses.

These realizations lead to the observation that we use two modes of communication according to the two modes of sensibility: one for and by the body, and one for and by the intellect; one outward and one inward. Moreover, each of these domains of communication has its prototypical media of communication: for the outward, our technologies, beginning with speech; for the inward, prayer and the sacraments. But that is not all. There is an additional dimension to man's *sensus communis*, consisting of the group faith, hope, and charity. Each of the theological virtues acts as a sense, a way of knowing. And as they are an acknowledged group, they must have a common sense. For example, begin with the notion that faith is a way of knowing. Each of the three theological virtues, faith, hope, and charity, is a way of knowing; that is, each is a sense, a modality of experience. The theological virtues are an acknowledged set of senses, theological senses. As Pope John Paul II comments in *Crossing the Threshold of Hope*:

> *Carmelite mysticism begins at the point where the reflections of Buddha end*, together with his instructions for the spiritual life. In the active and passive purification of the human soul, in those specific nights of the senses and the spirit, Saint John of the Cross sees, above all, the preparation for the human soul necessary to be permeated with the living flame of love. And this is also the title of his major work—*The Living Flame of Love*.
>
> Therefore, despite similar aspects, there is a fundamental difference. Christian mysticism from every period—beginning with the era of the Fathers of the Eastern and Western Church, to the great theologians of scholasticism (such as Saint Thomas Aquinas), to the northern European mystics, to the

Carmelite mystics—is not born of a purely negative "enlightenment." It is not born of an awareness of the evil which exists in man's attachment to the world through the senses, the intellect and the spirit.[107] Instead, Christian mysticism is born of the *Revelation of the living God*. This God opens himself to union with man, arousing in him the capacity to be united with him, especially by means of the theological virtues—faith, hope, and, above all, love.[108]

These theological senses, tightly interlinked, make up an ecological group as completely a *sensus communis* as the two groups we have been discussing thus far. Charity/love is the foundation for the set, the one that, in a way, includes the other sets:

> Peoples and nations of the entire world need to hear these words ["Be not afraid"]. Their conscience needs to grow in the certainty that Someone exists who holds in his hands the destiny of this passing world; Someone who holds the keys to death and the netherworld (cf. Rev 1:18); Someone who is the Alpha and the Omega of human history (cf. Rev 22:13)—be it the individual or collective history. And this Someone is Love (cf. 1 John 4:8, 16)—Love that became man, Love crucified and risen. Love unceasingly present among men. It is Eucharistic Love. It is the infinite source of communion. He alone can give the ultimate assurance when He says, "Be not afraid!"[109]

Like faith, hope is a way of knowing, a palpable sense of the presence of the future.

Because the Pope is a witness of Christ and a minister of the Good News, he is a man of joy and a *man of hope, a man of the fundamental affirmation of the value of existence, the value of creation and of hope in the future life.* Naturally, this is neither a naïve joy nor a vain hope. The joy of the victory over evil does not obfuscate—it actually intensifies—*the realistic awareness of the existence of evil* in the world and in every man. The Gospel teaches us to call good and evil by name, but it also teaches: "Do not be conquered by evil but conquer evil with good" (cf. Rom 12:21).

Here Christian morality is fully expressed. If this morality, however, strives towards values, if it brings a universal affirmation of good, *it can be nothing but extraordinarily demanding.* Good, in fact, is not easy, it is always the "hard road" of which Christ speaks in the Gospel (cf. Mt. 7:14). Therefore, *the joy of good and the hope of its triumph* in man and in the world do not exclude fear for this good, for the disappearance of this hope.[110]

Pope John Paul II further emphasizes that hope embraces not only our ultimate salvation but also the resurrection of the body:

You will remember that my first encyclical on the Redeemer of man (*Redemptor Hominis*) appeared a few months after my election on October 16, 1978. This means that I was actually carrying its contents within me. I had only to "copy" from memory and experience what I had already been living on the threshold of the papacy.

I emphasize this because the encyclical represents a confirmation, on the one hand, of the *tradition of the schools* from which I came and, on the other hand, of the *pastoral style*, reflected in this encyclical. The Council proposed, especially in *Gaudium et Spes*, that the mystery of redemption should be seen in light of the great renewal of man and of all that is human. The encyclical aims to *be a great hymn of joy for the fact that man has been redeemed through Christ*—redeemed in spirit and in body. This redemption of the body subsequently found its own expression in the series of catecheses for the Wednesday Papal audiences: *"Male and Female He Created Them."* Perhaps it would be better to say: "male and female he redeemed them."[111]

The hope of which John Paul II speaks is no wistful desire, no wishful thinking, but, as he says, a certainty:

> Christianity *is a religion of salvation—a soteriological religion, to use the theological term*. Christian soteriology focuses on the Paschal Mystery. In order to hope for salvation from God, man must stop beneath Christ's Cross. Then, the Sunday after the Holy Sabbath, he must stand in front of the empty tomb and listen, like the women of Jerusalem: "He is not here, for he has been raised" (Mt. 28:6). Contained within the Cross and Resurrection is the certainty that God saves man, that He saves him through Christ, through His Cross and His Resurrection.[112]

The three theological virtues have been yoked together from the first: St. Paul speaks of them as a unit, as "these three."[113] It remains only to add that they are senses, and not passive senses but active powers of the soul. But do they actually form a separate *sensus communis*?

Simply ask the question, to which of the other common senses might the theological virtues belong? Clearly, they are not bodily senses on the order of hearing and touch; neither do they belong with the group of intellectual senses. Equally clearly, though, they penetrate those two kinds of *sensus communis* and communicate with and through them, yet they are separate and distinct. Ergo, they constitute a *sensus communis* of their own. Pope Francis writes:

> Suffering reminds us that faith's service to the common good is always one of hope—a hope which looks ever ahead in the knowledge that only from God, from the future which comes from the risen Jesus, can our society find solid and lasting foundations. In this sense faith is linked to hope, for even if our dwelling place here below is wasting away, we have an eternal dwelling place which God has already prepared in Christ, in his body (cf. 2 Cor 4:16-5:5). The dynamic of faith, hope, and charity (cf. 1 Th 1:13; 1 Cor 13:13) thus leads us to embrace the concerns of all men on our journey toward that city "whose architect and builder is God" (Heb 11:10), for "hope does not disappoint" (Rom 5:5).
>
> In union with faith and charity, hope propels us toward a sure future, set against a different horizon with regard to the illusory enticements of the

idols of this world yet granting new momentum and strength to our daily lives. Let us refuse to be robbed of hope or to allow our hope to be dimmed by facile answers and solutions which block our progress, "fragmenting" time and changing it into space. Time is always much greater than space. Space hardens processes, whereas time propels toward the future and encourages us to go forward in hope.[114]

The human common sense is one thing, not three things; one thing with three dimensions: corporal, intellectual, and theological. The human soul apparently enjoys the same unity and dimensionality of physical, intellectual, and spiritual faculties. Like the soul, the *sensus communis* is not a compound of disparate elements but a threefold unity: each of its dimensions remains distinct, asserting its own character while in full interplay with the others. The immortal soul animates the mortal body and confers on it its humanity. It performs the same service for the intellect, so it may be considered the ground for both.[115]

We have also learned that the first two modes of *sensus communis* are in constant interplay and affect each other, for the soul is the form of the body and gives it its life.

2. ...it seems sufficiently clear that the "experience of the body," as we can gather from the ancient text of Genesis 2:23 and even more so of Genesis 2:25, indicates a degree of spiritualization of man that differs from the one about which the text speaks after original sin (Gen 3) and which we know from the experience of "historical" man. It is a different

measure of "spiritualization" that implies another composition of inner forces in man himself, another body-soul relation, as it were, other inner proportions between sensitivity, spirituality, and affectivity, that is, another degree of inner sensibility for the gifts of the Holy Spirit.[116]

Consequently, besides that of the theological virtues, there are involved two distinct but complementary ecologies, an ecology of the body and its senses, and an ecology of intellectual sensing. And the two ecologies are in constant conversation and affect each other.

> In dealing with the sacrifice of the new law in which the Church offers herself at the same time as she offers Christ, [Ivo of Chartres] portrays her made ready by previous rites to carry out this high office: *per aquam baptismatis adjunct, charismatis oleo peruncta, sancti Spiritus igne solidata, per humilitatis Spiritum hostia placens effecta*,[117] so that through each one of us this one Church ever appears as the chief object as well as the chief minister of all the sacraments. *Sacramenta faciunt ecclesiam*.[118]
>
> The efficacy of penance is explained like that of baptism, for the relationship is quite as clear, in the case of the former, between sacramental forgiveness and the social reintegration of the sinner. The double functions of this sacrament as a disciplinary institution and as a means of inner purification are not merely associated in fact; they are united, if one may so put it, by the nature of things.[119]

It becomes clear, then, that man employs two modes of communication: one, consisting of man-made technologies, which we now call the media, and including languages; and one consisting of the sacraments given to us by God and administered by the Church. And the two modes of communication do affect each other in subtle and surprising ways.

> Man appears in the visible world as the highest expression of the divine gift, because he bears within himself the inner dimension of the gift. And with it he carries into the world his particular likeness to God, with which he transcends and also rules his "visibility" in the world, his bodiliness, his masculinity or femininity, his nakedness. A reflection of this likeness is also the primordial awareness of the spousal meaning of the body pervaded by the mystery of original innocence.
>
> 4. Thus, in this dimension, a primordial sacrament is constituted, understood as a *sign that efficaciously transmits in the visible world the invisible mystery hidden in God from eternity.* And this is the mystery of Truth and Love, the mystery of divine life, in which man really participates. In the history of man, it is original innocence that begins this participation and is also the source of original happiness. The sacrament, as a visible sign, is constituted with man, inasmuch as he is a "body," though his "visible" masculinity and femininity. The body, in fact, and only the body, is capable of making visible what is invisible: the spiritual and the divine. It has been created to transfer into the visible reality of the world the

mystery hidden from eternity in God, and thus to be a sign of it.

5. In man, created in the image of God, the very sacramentality of creation, the sacramentality of the world, was thus in some way revealed. In fact, through his bodiliness, his masculinity and femininity, man becomes a visible sign of the economy of Truth and love, which has its source in God himself and was revealed already in the mystery of creation. Against this vast background, we fully understand the words in Genesis 2:24 that are constitutive of the sacrament of marriage: "For this reason a man will leave his father and his mother and unite with his wife, and the two will be one flesh." Against this vast background we also understand that, through the whole depth of their anthropological meaning, the words of Genesis 2:25 ("Both were naked, the man and his wife, but they did not feel shame") expresses the fact that, *together with man, holiness has entered the visible world*, the world created for him. The sacrament of the world, and the sacrament of man in the world, comes forth from the divine source of holiness and is instituted, at the same time, for holiness. Original innocence, connected with the experience of the spousal meaning of the body, is holiness itself, which permits man to express himself deeply with his own body, precisely through the "sincere gift" of self (*Gaudium et Spes*, 24:3). Consciousness of the gift conditions in this case "the sacrament of the body": in his body as man or woman, man senses himself as a subject of holiness.[120]

For each of these domains of communication, the inward and the outward, there is a prototype.

The prototypical technology of bodily communication is language and speech, which we use to converse with one another and as well to pray, to converse with heaven. That is to say that the etymology of all of our media is to be found in the matrix and pattern of speech and language. These matters form the fundamental theme of our study *Laws of Media: The New Science*.[121] In that book, we show that every technology, every human innovation, whether of a tangible, hardware kind or whether made of information or ideas (software) is a form of utterance and has its etymology in the human body and its faculties. Furthermore, we examine the four modes of etymology—of our utterances and inventions of every kind—in detail in *The Human Equation* series of books.[122]

Alone among forms of writing, the phonetic alphabet was powerful enough to suppress *mimesis* and break the spell under which the poets held dominion over oral culture. For the alphabet gave the Greeks their first experience of detachment and objectivity, essential to establishing abstract thought. Objectivity and detachment also led directly to private, individual identity inasmuch as they are correlatives of a separation of knower and known, and thus also separation of the individual from identification with and participation in the group. Such dissociation of sensibilities meant a radical bias imposed upon the bodily *sensus communis* in which the visual sense was to reign over the household of the senses for the next two millennia.[123] The alphabet literally paved the way for our doctrines of individual responsibility (and the sacrament of penance) and individual salvation. For salvation during Old Testament times had been of and by the group: the Jews were a chosen *people*, not a collection of private individuals.

In our time, the return of *mimesis* was heralded by artists and poets such as Baudelaire with his rallying cry, "*Hypocrite lecteur!*" He was not in advance of his time; he was simply in advance of his contemporaries.[124] T. S. Eliot spelled out the dynamics of this situation when he discussed the meaning of Dante both to the Middle Ages and to our time:

> ...I may say that the great poet should not only perceive and distinguish more clearly than other men, the colours or sounds within the range of ordinary vision and hearing; he should perceive vibrations beyond the range of ordinary men, and be able to make men see and hear more at each end [of the spectrum] than they could ever see without his help. We have for instance in English literature great religious poets, but they are, by comparison with Dante, *specialists*. That is all they can do. And Dante, because he could do everything else, is for that reason the greatest "religious" poet, though to call him a "religious poet" would be to abate his universality. *The Divine Comedy* expresses everything in the way of emotion, between depravity's despair and the beatific vision, that man is capable of experiencing. It is therefore a constant reminder to the poet, of the obligation to explore, to find words for the inarticulate, to capture those feelings which people can hardly even feel, because they have no words for them; and at the same time, a reminder that the explorer beyond the frontiers of ordinary consciousness will only be able to return and report to his fellow-citizens, if he has all the time a firm

grasp upon the realities with which they are already acquainted.[125]

Evidently, Baudelaire and the Symbolists were making their raids on the inarticulate. In the same vein, Pablo Neruda, by general consent Walt Whitman's truest heir, said that the appeal of Whitman to the Spanish poets was that "he taught how to see and name what had not been seen and named before":

> Poetry in South America is a different matter altogether. You see there are in our countries rivers which have no names, trees which nobody knows, and birds which nobody has described. It is easier for us to be surrealistic because everything we know is new... Our duty, then, as we understand it, is to express what is unheard of. Everything has been painted in Europe, everything has been sung in Europe. But not in America. In that sense, Whitman was a great teacher. Because what is Whitman? He was not only intensely conscious, but he was open-eyed! he had tremendous eyes to see everything—he taught us to see things. He was our poet.[126]

The return of *mimesis* to Western sensibility brings with it a suspension of detachment and objectivity that were introduced by the alphabet—that, after all, is the principal implication of "*Hypocrite lecteur!*" The erasure of detachment means the gradual erasure of individual identity and of private responsibility as group participatory forms reassert themselves. As private identity is inextricably linked to private goals and private ambitions, they, too, are fast disappearing from the Western mindset. All of these movements are well under way in our culture, and have been at least since the first Vatican Council, which may be seen, at least in part, as a response to the new conditions. The implications for the sacraments are obvious, and everywhere to be seen manifest in our time. But what provoked these counter-cultural movements? If the phonetic alphabet, with its message of detached individualism, paved the way for the New Testament, with its message of individual salvation, for what are these new developments paving the way?

Beginning in the nineteenth century, we introduced new forms of communication: electric technologies such as the telegraph and the telephone and, soon after them, the radio. Unlike earlier hardware technologies, these new forms operate at speeds approaching that of light, virtually instantaneously. Older forms of communication, such as speech and writing, move goods and information at speeds commensurate with human scale.

At electric speeds, there is no movement of information or idea from place to place or from person to person; there is no human scale. If you will, the "message" does not move from here to there; it is the sender that is sent, minus his physical body. *In effect.* The audience ("receiver") performs a complementary maneuver and is suddenly everywhere at the same time. Both parties are simply, suddenly, and unexpectedly present everywhere. The physical body no longer constitutes a limiting factor. On the telephone or on the air or online, the disincarnated user is simultaneously here and there at the same time. The user can be in two places at the same time, or two dozen places, or two million: *there is no difference.* For some generations now we have been calling this condition "the mass audience." For the mass audience, there is no movement to or from, just simultaneity of being. This is *a new experience of being*; this separation from the body and its constraints. The new media, then, are not manifestations of physical communication so much as manifestations of *meta*physical communication. They entail the transformation of the users. Twentieth-century man—electronic man—has now lived minus a physical body for an entire century. He has become *dis*incarnate and has become accustomed to substituting an abstract image for his physical being. The telephone is the most obvious prototype of these *discarnating instruments, and underpins all the effects that go with the discarnate state*. Discarnate man has no relation to natural law, and thus has no private identity and no relation to natural morality.

Aquinas avers repeatedly that the principle of individuation is the joining of a material body and a spirit, a soul. His usual term is *materia signata*, matter signed with spirit. The soul is the animating principle for the body, and it makes the body human.

> Accordingly, in the world of physical objects, matter does not of itself participate in actual existence; but it does participate therein through form; for the form coming upon the matter makes the matter itself actually exist, as the soul does to the body.[127]

But what happens when the two, body and soul, are sundered by technology, however briefly? in terms of the corporal *sensus communis*, the effect is to remove the ground that supports individual identity, private identity. The recourse then is to seek identity in the group, and there are a multitude of group-participatory experiences available on the internet, not the least of which are the many role-playing games.[128]

But people who participate routinely in the discarnate experience insist that they experience a strong feeling of individualism. How is one to account for that? The common perception today of uniqueness may perhaps come about as a parody of the condition of the angels: minus a body, each angel is a separate species. In article eight of the *Disputed Questions on Spiritual Creatures*, St. Thomas asks "whether all angels differ in species from one another." He decides there are three reasons to affirm that they do so differ:

> But in the higher part of the universe a higher degree of perfection is found, wherein one individual being... is so perfect that it lacks none of the things that pertain to its own species, and hence also the whole matter of the species is contained in one individual being... Much more so, therefore, this perfection is found in the highest part of created things which is nearest to God, namely, among the angels: that one individual lacks none of the things which pertain to a whole species, and thus there are not several individuals in one species.[129]

So there actually are as many species of angels as there are angels. That is not true of humans, of course, as each discarnate person does have a body somewhere offstage, but the sense of uniqueness, the perception thereof, might possibly be due to the temporary condition of disembodiment. The language used, typically, in these and kindred matters is that of the previous (now obsolescent) state,[130] so disembodiment is called individualism although it is nothing like individualism, that is, private identity.

The moral anarchy of our time is directly related to our technologies as formal influences *and does not result from the uses to which the technologies are put.* These facts are totally overlooked by the commentators on the impact of the telephone and the others. The content of the telephone, the radio, TV, computer, or satellite, etc., serves precisely the same function as the "meaning of a poem" discussed earlier: it keeps the mind occupied while the technology does its work on the user, unhindered.

Technological modifications of the body or the sensory order have corresponding effects on the *sensus communis*: among them is a distinct weakening of the sense of faith.

> It must be remembered that from the earliest times of Christianity there appears a permanent and unrelinquishable "nucleus" of catechesis, hence of formation in the faith. Luther also employed this nucleus for his catechism, in the same matter-of-fact way as did the Roman catechism that had been decided upon at the Council of Trent. All that is said about faith, after all, is organized around four fundamental elements: the *Credo*, the *Our Father*, the *Decalogue*, the *sacraments*. These embrace the foundation of Christian life, the synthesis of the teaching of the Church based on Scripture and Tradition. Here the Christian finds all that he must *believe* (the Symbol or Credo), *hope* (the Our Father), *do* (the Decalogue) as well as the vital space (*Lebensraum*) in which all this must be accomplished (the sacraments). Today this fundamental structure is neglected in extensive areas of present-day catechesis. The result, as we note, has

been a disintegration of the *sensus fidei* in the new generations who are often incapable of a comprehensive review of their religion.[131]

It has long been an axiom of understanding media that each new medium or technology of communication, each extension of man, introduces a new form of awareness, a new configuration of the *sensus communis*. The most recent test of these notions comes from scientific comparison of two kinds of writing:[132] The phonetic alphabet and Chinese characters:

> There are few more powerful mirrors of the human brain's astonishing ability to rearrange itself to learn a new intellectual function than the act of reading. Underlying the brain's ability to learn reading lies its protean capacity to make new connections among structures and circuits originally devoted to other more basic brain processes that have enjoyed a longer existence in human evolution, such as vision and spoken language. We now know that groups of neurons create new connections and pathways among themselves every time we acquire a new skill. Computer scientists use the term "open architecture" to describe a system that is versatile enough to change—or rearrange—to accommodate the varying demands on it. Within the constraints of our genetic legacy, our brain presents a beautiful example of open architecture… Reading can be learned only because of the brain's plastic design, and when reading takes place, that individual brain is forever changed,[133] both physiologically and intellectually.

> For example, at the neuronal level, a person who learns to read in Chinese uses a very particular set of neuronal connections that differ in significant ways from the pathways used in reading English. When Chinese readers first try to read in English, their brains attempt to use Chinese-based neuronal pathways. The act of learning to read Chinese characters has literally shaped the Chinese reading brain. Similarly much of how we think and what we think about is based on insights and associations generated from what we read.[134]

Note that there is here no discussion of the content of the writing system. Attention is focused on the system itself and the configuration of sensibilities that it brings to the user. ("Open architecture" applies to the *sensus communis* of the body and to that of the intellect, but not that of the theological virtues: they do not "grow" as do the physical or mental faculties.) This suggests why the missionaries were compelled to take with them the alphabet: they used it to prepare the ground for converting non-literate populations. Half a century before Maryanne Wolf performed her researches, Jacques Ellul (of whom she is unaware) examined in detail the effects of media of propaganda and observed that the two things (media and propaganda) had separate, and separable, effects:

> One must also distinguish between different effects produced by different media. Each has its own effects on attitudes or opinions, whether the propagandist purposely provokes them or not. When a man goes to the movies, he receives certain

impressions, and his inner life is modified independently of all propaganda. Such psychological effects or changes of opinion, specific to each of the communications media, join those specifically produced by propaganda operations. To analyze where one ends and the other begins is very difficult.[135]

Although Ellul here is talking of political propaganda, what he says applies directly to the effort to propagate the faith among non-literate populations:

> Propaganda cannot succeed where people have no trace of Western culture. We are not speaking here of intelligence; some primitive tribes are surely intelligent, but have an intelligence foreign to our concepts and customs. A base is needed—for example, education; a man who cannot read will escape most propaganda, as will a man who is not interested in reading.[136]

Reading, he points out again and again, serves to separate the individual consciousness from the bond of the group. That is, alphabetic literacy; the rash of "literacies" in our time is another matter altogether. They involve a revival of *mimesis*.

David Booth shows *mimesis* at work today in the context of the new literacies: a routine educational procedure.

> When students are inside the experience, needing to read and write in order to come to grips with the issues and concerns being discussed or examined, when texts are being interpreted or constructed as

part of the learning process, then I can sense that a literacy event is happening. The young person needs not only to inhabit the words and images, but to see herself as a performer of what she has learned, representing and owning the learning. In effect, she herself becomes the literacy. And she reads and writes with her whole self, with her body, with her emotions, with her background as a daughter and student and citizen; she sits in school beside her family members, and she reads every text she meets alongside them, inside her cultural surround. Literacy is constructed through identity.[137]

An autistic reveals the same process: "My language is not about designing words or even visual symbols for people to interpret. It is about being in constant conversation with every aspect of my environment. Reacting to all parts of my surroundings."[138] Booth is describing a culture of children fully immersed in their sensory world, one that adults may find foreign, but which is increasingly a normal state for our children.

The effect of all of our electric technologies, taken together, is to restructure the human sensorium, the bodily *sensus communis* together with the intellectual *sensus communis*, into a configuration roughly *equivalent to their pattern before the Incarnation*. That is, the effects of the phonetic alphabet are reversed. The 2,500-year period of the alphabet and its influence is become a digression, or an incubation period, but for what? Why is this massive change taking place? The phonetic alphabet began in a particular part of the world and spread from there: it took eight centuries to conquer Greece and Rome and reigned for another twenty centuries before its displacement in our time.

The onset was gradual; the overthrow is sudden, by comparison: it has occupied a mere century and a half. The phonetic alphabet conquered one culture at a time; electric technologies now constitute global environments, not merely local ones. Every innovation now affects the entire globe at once.

The physical body of the disincarnated user is still there, tucked away somewhere, in one of the locations, but it is irrelevant to the new condition of multi-locationalism. The point is that man is now split; he lives two lives, one in the body and one out of the body. The natural integrity of the body has been set aside, and the bodily *sensus communis* is in disarray, disintegrated. Or is it more accurate to say that the dissociated sensibility given us by the phonetic alphabet has been yanked back together by our electric technologies?

A reintegration is not a restoration of the original form. For that, one would have to abstain from all technologies for decades, or, more probably, for several generations. The structure of awareness, too, is changing. The phonetic alphabet had institutionalized the subconscious by introducing elements of the process of reading that were to remain out of conscious awareness: for example, the reader is not to be aware of individual letters as he reads, or of the words on the pages as artifacts, as words. Nor is he to be aware of the page as such. He is trained to devote all his attention to the play of meanings. Reading is cerebral. We all have had the experience: when rapt in a text, everything fades from our awareness—all but the narrative. It absorbs every available shred of attention; the rest we relegate to the subconscious, even the people and sounds and events in the reader's immediate surroundings.[139] In the ancient world, only the phonetic alphabet was powerful enough to cast this spell: it was not possible with any of the syllabaries, all of which necessitated constant attention to the characters and diacritical marks to decide proper meanings and sounds from a field of possibilities. Today, the situation has shifted from a separate conscious and unconscious or subconscious to various forms of reintegration of the two. One such contemporary example is called multi-tasking. Another is interactive multimedia. Another, postliteracy.

In the West, the onset of postliteracy began when *mimesis* reappeared in the arts; when, that is, detachment was breached. Fifty years ago, postliteracy was being widely noticed. Today, we are surrounded by people who know how to read but who prefer not to: reading is too taxing; it is hard work. Prose styles have changed to accommodate the new sensibilities. Sentence length in popular writing has shortened drastically to suit abbreviated attention spans; the developed paragraph is largely a thing of the past. That is, average sentence length varies now between eight and twelve words, and average paragraph length between one and four sentences. Attention span, a function of the *sensus communis*, relates directly to life "in the now," as much as to deferred gratification ("futurology" is the future regarded as an art form). A separate indicator: the drastic shortening of broadcast advertisements. A generation ago, the one-minute television advertisement was the norm; now thirty-second ads seem over-long, and much briefer ones—fifteen-second ones, or ten-and even five-second ads—are becoming so common as to be unremarkable. One American news network has begun using two-second ads to promote its news shows and features. And advertisers have discovered the great advantage of the five-second ad: the viewer does not have time to ignore it.[140]

With electricity, the sender, not the information, is sent; the receiver is also sent, in metaphysical reciprocity. Electric media belong to the domain of metaphysics, not that of physics: in the world of simultaneity, the emphasis shifts automatically from *becoming* to sheer *being*. Being, that is, *in the now*; for sequential time (the *sine qua non* of becoming) is also rendered obsolescent as a mode of experience. Does this not constitute an undermining of the theological virtue of hope? For how does one look forward to a future or hope for or plan a future in a world of simultaneous time, where future and past are gathered together in the present? We can see evidences that this condition prevails here on every hand, whenever we hear of being or living "in the now"—a constant refrain in advertising, to mention just one area. "In the now" also underlies the new need for newscasts composed of "breaking news"; that is, news coverage of events as they occur, even before they have been declared to be news! Instant coverage throws the audience onto the scene, amidst the action "in real time," to cater to heightened desires for participation—and to set aside as much detachment, objectivity, and reflection as possible. The aim of news realigns from reportage to providing an experience.

Films now emphasize the *experience* of the film where formerly they placed emphasis on the narrative, the story, the development of character and situation. Now, there is little or no development: development is foreign to television shows. Film soundtracks are delivered at high volume, too high to be listened to, but high enough that the *feeling* of the sounds is foregrounded. Special effects are all the rage…

In recreational games, the emphasis is now on playing roles (*mimesis*) and on fantasy. Fantasy and dreams are worlds apart. Dreams relate to a future time; dreams entail deferred gratification; fantasies are their own reward; fantasies live in a here and now. One who lives in the here and now has little use for deferred gratification: he lives life immersed in being, a condition with little use for becoming.

The emphasis on and social acceptance of living in the here and now signals a deep disturbance in the ecology of the Western intellect; it has several associated symptoms. One is the relative disappearance of long-range goals, particularly among the young. As mentioned, this aspect of living "in the now" undercuts as well the theological virtue of hope, the expectation of eventual salvation, and of the resurrection of the body. Another malaise is the widespread disinclination to grow up, reinforced by constant injunctions that older people (older, that is, than "the young") remain youthful in appearance and demeanour. In support we find a vast array of chemicals and cosmetic surgical interventions to alter or adjust the body and its appearance: everything from facelifts (etc.) to breast surgery or liposuction. The institutionalization of immaturity strikes at the young, who naturally are inclined to want to grow up, and it undermines also the normal adult sense of responsibility. Hence, people are far less inclined to take seriously sin and its consequences, and the need for the sacrament of penance is diminished.

Numerous studies in the twentieth century bear on institutionalized immaturity directly or indirectly. E.g., Neil Postman's 1982 study *The Disappearance of Childhood*. As evidence for the disappearance, immediately following the introduction of television in 1950, he cites the rise of crime perpetrated by and against children; the increase in sexual activity and drug/alcohol abuse in children; children and adults sharing musical tastes, language, literature, and movies (many big budget movies are comic books that years earlier would have been marketed solely to children); the lack of differentiated clothing styles (little girls in high heels, grown men in sneakers). Even childhood games were replaced by organized sports (Little League, Pee Wee, etc.) that are more like adult sports. "Adulthood has lost much of its authority and aura, and the idea of deference to one who is older has become ridiculous."[141] The artist and writer Wyndham Lewis (one of the "moderns," alongside T. S. Eliot, W. B. Yeats, Ezra Pound, and James Joyce), penned *Doom of Youth* in 1932: in it he argues that once we stop believing in an afterlife there is no reward later, only youth *now*. In *Doom*, Lewis probes the consequences of the adult refusal to grow up. What happens, he asked, when older folk refuse to leave the nursery behind? He concludes that the results would be catastrophic for children, and events (e.g., abortion) have proven him right.[142]

> Really what the "Doom of Youth" means is the erecting of "Youth" into a unique value, and by so doing abolishing Youth altogether. For something that is *everything* in human life cannot be anything so limited as "Youth" as understood upon the merely emotional plane.
> A "Youth" (Peter Pan) that never can grow up—that is the all-youth of the super-sentimentalist. For him there is nothing in the world of any value but "youth" in the traditionally romantic, the sugar-and-spice sense. "Youth-politician"—that is diametrically the opposite to Sir James Barrie's sickly variety, or the bogus and lisping species that is peculiar to the invert's paradise.
> For the "Youth-politician" there is, strictly speaking, no youth. There are only different degrees and powers of an abstract energy. There is one long *adult*

life, if you like. No life is worth considering, for the "Youth-politician," except adult life. And adult life is not worthwhile, of course, once the person is no longer active and capable of creative or at least of useful work...

It is quite clear what is intended, and what is destined to come about. "Youth" is to be abolished altogether (just as the old "sex" conception was wiped out by Feminism). And it is also quite certain that it is the very reverse of that to the mind of the Everymans that is on foot: nothing but endless, irresponsible, something-for-nothing "Youth" is their *simplest* of "Youth-politics." And of course, for the *Everymans* it *will* be the reverse.[143]

In a chapter reporting on "The Position of the Cult of the Child in the Present System," Lewis remarks:

> I will interpolate here a brief account of how the child cult should be placed politically in relation to the attack on the family unit and the sex war. If you explained it entirely on the score of a defeated vitality, or of political eclipse, you would be mistaken, I think.
>
> The contributing causes of the cult of the child... could be capitulated as follows: (1) its usefulness as a kind of defeatist paradise for most of those accepting it: (2) its role as a factor in the "sex war": and (3) its usefulness to those responsible for it and to some extent imposing it. It is obvious how closely it is related in that case with the wave of masculine inversion.[144]

Today's refusal to mature doesn't stem from laziness: it is a way to make time to adjust to current cultural conditions in flux. However, it is worth noting that if healthy people are those who continue to grow and to mature throughout their lives, those that don't are, in effect, dead. Christopher Lasch wrote that "the distinction between the self and the not-self is the basis of all other distinctions, including the distinction between life and death... The narcissistic longing for fusion leads to a denial of both sexual and generational differences."[145]

Why, exactly, should a grown person wish to remain a child—for to use the forms of infantile or immature life, to make an art of its technical imperfections and to exploit its natural ignorance, are, in some sense to wish to be a child. A year after writing *The Art of Being Ruled*, Lewis said:

> How the demented also joins hands with the child, and the tricks, often very amusing, of the asylum patient, are exploited at the same time as the happy inaccuracies of the infant; how contemporary inverted-sex fashions are affiliated to the Child-cult; and in fact all the different factors in this intricate sensibility, being evolved notably by such writers as Miss [Gertrude] Stein, will be found there. not to seize the secret of these liaisons is to totally misunderstand the nature of what is occurring around you today.[146]

That was in 1927; it might have been said last year. In a recent book, Diana West points out that "a state of exposure—not innocence—now coincides with the earliest stirrings of self-awareness that usually begin with life after" the nursery:

Twenty years ago, Dartmouth College made shocking headlines for equipping college freshmen not just with everything they needed to know about sex, but rather everything they needed to engage in it... along with various examples of drugstore birth control, the freshman sex kit includes an "oral dam"... Back then, a college setting up eighteen-year-olds for sexual experimentation seemed outrageous. Today, middle school students in Maryland learn "buying a condom is not as scary as you think." In Wisconsin, they can pick them up for free at a "health" fair. First-graders in North Carolina get primed on homosexual marriage with *King and King*, a story book about a handsome prince who spurns a run of princesses for a handsome prince of his own. New Jersey put together a sex ed kit that, among other things, gives elementary school students, the lowdown on masturbation. Kindergarteners in New York learn the mechanics of AIDS transmission.

What happened to innocence? No longer considered a boon to virtuous behavior, innocence—of drugs, of sex, of homosexual princes, and of oral dams—is today deemed a handicap, an affliction to be cured as quickly as possible. Intensive treatment takes place both in the classroom and through the culture. Meanwhile the notion of virtue itself—"conformity to a standard of right," Webster's says—is out altogether, replaced by the multifarious "values" of a relativistic culture. By definition, these values conform to *no* standard of right.[147]

These practices, spreading quickly through the culture, could be seen as a frontal attack on the sacraments, particularly the sacrament of marriage. In our time, children have little incentive to grow up. Once, they were motivated by a desire to enter the adult world and participate in its enjoyments and freedoms and responsibilities; today, the child has unrestricted access to all things once considered the adult preserve. He and she see the same programs and films, use the same internet and services. It is usual that children play with new technologies and develop expertise with them long before their elders access them. In terms of experience, the only significant difference between children and adults is the state of physical development, and in an environment of discarnate experience that difference carries little weight. On the air, on the telephone, on the internet, in "cyberspace," there is no young or old or male or female. These are *in*carnate categories.

Pope Francis observes:

> The sacraments communicate an incarnate memory, linked to the times and places of our lives, linked to all our senses; in them the whole person is engaged as a member of a living subject and part of a network of communitarian relationships. While the sacraments are indeed sacraments of faith,[148] it can also be said that faith itself possesses a sacramental structure. The awakening of faith is linked to the dawning of a new sacramental sense in our lives as men and as Christians, in which visible and material realities are seen to point beyond themselves to the mystery of the eternal.[149]

For orientation, recall the central fact that the soul animates the body and makes it human; without the body the human being is, to say the least, profoundly disoriented, and perhaps somewhat less than human. John Paul II anticipates the thoughts offered by Pope Francis:

> 7. In the prophetic texts, the human body speaks a *"language"* of which it is not the author. *Its author is man*, as male or female, as bridegroom or bride: man with his perennial vocation to the communion of persons. Yet, man is *in some sense unable to express* this singular language of his personal existence and vocation *without the body*. He is constituted in such a way from the "beginning" that the deepest words of the spirit—words of love, gift, and faithfulness—call for an appropriate "language of the body." And without this language, they cannot be fully expressed. We know from the gospel that this point applies both to marriage and to continence "for the kingdom of heaven."
>
> 8. Through this "language of the body," the prophets, as the inspired spokesmen of Yahweh's covenant with Israel, attempt to express both the spousal depth of that covenant and all that contradicts it. They sing the praises of faithfulness and stigmatize unfaithfulness as "adultery": they speak thus according to ethical categories setting moral good and evil in mutual opposition. The antithesis of good and evil is essential for ethos. The prophetic texts have in this sphere an essential significance, as

we emphasized already in our earlier reflections.[150] It seems, however, that the "language of the body" according to the prophets is not only a language of ethos, not only a song of praise for faithfulness and purity as well as a condemnation of "adultery" and "prostitution." In fact, inasmuch as every language is an expression of knowledge, the categories of truth and untruth (or falsity) are essential for it. In the texts of the prophets, who see marriage in the analogy of Yahweh's covenant with Israel, *the body tells the truth* through faithfulness and conjugal love, and, when it commits "adultery" it tells a lie, it *commits falsehood*.

9. The point is not to replace ethical differentiations by logical ones. When the prophetic texts point to conjugal faithfulness and chastity as "truth" and to adultery, by contrast, as un-truth, as "falsity" in the language of the body, they do so because in the first case the subject (Israel as bride) agrees with the spousal meaning that corresponds to the human body (because of its masculinity or femininity) in the integral structure of the person; in the second case, by contrast, the same subject finds itself in contradiction against, and in collision with, that meaning.[151]

Most of the effects of the discarnate environment strike at the roots of sacramental marriage: because sacramental marriage insists on the body and the language of the body, the flourishing discarnate state weakens our attachment to marriage and weakens our understanding of what the sacrament means. We no longer accept as givens the blanket assumptions of incarnate existence; we do incline toward those of cyberlife. If, as he has just remarked, "We can say that the essential element for marriage as a sacrament is the 'language of the body' reread in the truth" and "it is precisely through this that the sacramental sign is constituted," then that language of the body and all that depends on it are in peril in an era when the body can be doffed or donned with the insouciant abandon we commonly exhibit. In the body and out of it—each condition calls for a different posture of the *sensus communis*, or for a modified *sensus communis*. There is no evidence whatsoever to suggest that frequent moving back and forth from one state to the other is any better for the psyche than frequent moving in and out of air conditioning during summer months in a hot climate is good for the body. Can one or another *sensus communis* catch a cold, as it were?

All that is necessary to subvert the sacrament of marriage is simply to dissolve the bond between sexuality and motherhood. As Cardinal Ratzinger observes, "Separated from motherhood, sex has remained without a locus and has lost its point of reference: it is a kind of drifting mine, a problem and at the same time an omnipresent power."[152] Following this first rupture, he sees another:

> After the separation between sexuality and motherhood was effected, sexuality was also separated from procreation. The movement, however, ended up going in an opposite direction: procreation without sexuality. Out of this follow the increasingly shocking medical-technical experiments so prevalent in our day where, precisely, procreation is

independent of sexuality. Biological manipulation is striving to uncouple man from nature (the very existence of which is being disputed). There is an attempt to transform man, to manipulate him as one does every other "thing": he is nothing but a product planned according to one's pleasure.[153]

It seems clear that the sacrament of marriage, which Pope John Paul II identifies as the foundation of the sacramental system, is particularly vulnerable to the discarnate effect of our electric technologies. Cardinal Ratzinger "cites some trends" of the confusions this situation has wrought between the magisterium and theologians:

...at times, premarital relations, at least under certain conditions, are justified. Masturbation is presented as a normal phenomenon of adolescence. Admission of remarried divorced couples to the sacraments is constantly demanded. Radical feminism—especially in some women's religious orders—also seems to be gaining ground noticeably in the Church... even as regards the question of homosexuality, attempts at its justification are in the making. Indeed, it has come to pass that bishops—on the basis of insufficient information or also because of a sense of guilt among Catholics toward an "oppressed minority"—have placed churches at the disposal of *"gays"* for their gatherings. Then there is the case of *Humane Vitae*, the encyclical of Paul VI, which reaffirmed the "no" to contraceptives and which has not been understood.[154]

The prototypical sacrament is marriage, as John Paul repeatedly points out.

> 1. ...we spoke about the integral heritage of the covenant with God and about the grace originally united to the divine work of creation. Part of this integral heritage—as one can deduce from Ephesians 5:22-33—was marriage as the primordial sacrament, instituted from the "beginning" and linked with the sacrament of creation in its totality. The sacramentality of marriage is not only a *model and figure* of the sacrament of the Church (of Christ and the Church), but also constitutes an essential part of the new heritage, that of the sacrament of redemption with which the Church is endowed with Christ. Here one must go back once more to Christ's words in Matthew 19:3-9 (cf. Mk. 10:5-9), in which Christ, in responding to the question of the Pharisees about marriage and its specific character, *appeals only and exclusively to its original institution* by the Creator at the "beginning." As we reflect about the meaning of this answer in the light of Ephesians, especially Ephesians 5:22–33, we end up with a somehow double relation of marriage to the whole sacramental order that emerges from the very sacrament of redemption in the New Covenant.
>
> 2. As the primordial sacrament, marriage constitutes, on the one hand, the *figure* (and thus the likeness, the analogy) according to which the underlying, weight-bearing structure of the new economy

of salvation and the sacramental order is built, which springs from the spousal gracing that the Church receives from Christ with all the goods of redemption (one could say, using the words from the beginning of Ephesians, "with all spiritual blessings," Eph. 1:3). Thus, as the primordial sacrament marriage is assumed and inserted into the integral structure of the new sacramental economy, which has arisen from redemption *in the form, I would say, of a "prototype."* It is assumed and inserted, as it were, from its very basis. In the dialogue with the Pharisees (Mt. 19:3-9), Christ himself confirms first of all its existence. If we reflect deeply on this dimension, we have to conclude that all the sacraments of the New Covenant find their prototype in some way in the sacrament of marriage as the primordial sacrament...

3. However, the relation of marriage to the whole sacramental order, which has arisen from the Church's endowment with the benefits of redemption, is not limited only to the dimension of model. In his dialogue with the Pharisees (see Mt. 19), Christ not only confirms the existence of marriage instituted from the "beginning" by the Creator, but he declares *also that it is an integral part of the new sacramental economy.* Of the new order of salvific "signs" that draws its origin from the sacrament of redemption, just as the original economy emerged from the sacrament of creation; and in fact, Christ limits himself to the one and only sacrament, which was marriage instituted in the state of original justice

and innocence of man, created as male and female "in the image and likeness of God."[155]

Asked in what way the Bible and the tradition of interpretation attribute "equality" to women while simultaneously excluding her from the priesthood, John Paul responds:

> Certainly, but it is further necessary to get to the bottom of the demand that radical feminism draws from the widespread modern culture, namely the "trivialization" of sexual specificity that makes every role interchangeable between man and woman. When we were speaking of the crisis of traditional morality, I indicated a series of fatal ruptures: that, for example, between sexuality and procreation. Detached from the bond with fecundity, sex no longer appears to be a determined characteristic, as a radical and pristine orientation of the person. Male? Female? They are questions that for some are now viewed as obsolete, senseless, if not racist. The answer of current conformism is foreseeable: "whether one is male or female has little interest for us, we are all simply humans." This, in reality, has grave consequences even if at first it appears very beautiful and generous. It signifies, in fact, that sexuality is no longer rooted in anthropology; it means that sex is viewed as a simple role, interchangeable at one's pleasure.

A knowledge of the role in urging and distorting these matters of the effects of our technological extensions and the response of the *sensus communis* would go far toward elucidating the real source of the problems and possible approaches to their solution.

Notes

96 T. S. Eliot, *The Use of Poetry & the Use of Criticism, op. cit.*, p. 151.
97 Therefore if the reader is insensitive or stupid, the poem is a correspondingly poor performance or simply confusing. Responding to a question about the proper meaning of one of his poems, Eliot retorted, "A poem cannot mean something it doesn't mean to you."
98 *On Poetry and Poets*, pp. 22–23.
99 de Lubac, *op. cit.*, p. 8.
100 *Man and Woman He Created Them: A Theology of the Body, op. cit.*, pp. 460–61. Note particularly how the four senses penetrate and provide the structure of each paragraph.
101 *Ibid.*, p. 461.
102 *Ibid.*, pp. 142–43.
103 *Ibid.*, p. 143.
104 *Ibid.*, p. 164. These words bear the following footnote: "In the conception of the most ancient biblical books, the dualistic antithesis 'body-soul' does not appear. As pointed out already [*TOB* 8:4 (pp. 160–61)], one could speak rather of a complementary combination 'body-life.' The body is an expression of man's personhood and, though it does not completely exhaust this concept, one should understand it in biblical language as 'pars pro toto' [the part standing for the whole]; cf. 'neither flesh nor blood have revealed this to you but my Father' (Mt. 16:17), that is, no human being has revealed it to you."

105 "No one, in fact, ever hates his own flesh but he nourishes and cares for it, as Christ does with the Church, because we are members of his body. For this reason a man will leave his father and his mother and unite with his wife and the two will form one flesh. This mystery is great; I say this with reference to Christ and the Church" (Eph. 5:29–32). (John Paul's note.) Recall the habitual interchangeability, during the Middle Ages, of the words, "mystery" and "sacrament."

106 *Op. cit.*, p. 165.

107 Each of which has its proper *sensus communis*.

108 *Crossing the Threshold of Hope*, ed. Vittorio Messori (Milan: Arnoldo Mondadori Editiore; Toronto: Alfred A. Knopf, 1994), pp. 87–88.

109 *Ibid.*, pp. 221–22.

110 *Ibid.*, pp. 22–23.

111 *Ibid.*, pp. 48–49.

112 *Ibid.*, p. 68.

113 Cf. 1 Corinthians 13:1–13.

114 *The Light of Faith (Lumen Fidei), op. cit.*, pp. 105–107.

115 At this point, one is tempted to inquire about the angels. Does an angel, too, have a *sensus communis*? Since an angel is a created spirit without a body, it will not have physical (corporal) senses, but it does have an immortal soul and an intellect. Of what might an angel's intellectual *sensus communis* consist? Or its theological *sensus communis*? Certainly an angel would have an abundance of faith and of love; but hope? The matter merits some consideration, if only for the light it may shed on the human condition.

116 *Op. cit.*, pp. 198–99.

117 "Conjoined by the waters of baptism, anointed by the

oil of chrism. Consolidated by the fire of the Holy Spirit, made into a pleasing host by the Spirit of Humility. *De convenientia veteris et novi Sacrificii* (PL 162, 544)." De Lubac's note, in part.

118   Sacraments make the Church. Cf. Pseudo-Haymo, *In Psalmos* (PL 116 248D).

119   de Lubac, *Catholicism: Christ and the Common Destiny of Man*, tr. Lancelot C. Sheppard and Sr. Elizabeth Englund, OCD (San Francisco: Ignatius Press, 1988), pp. 86–87.

120   *Man and Woman He Created Them: A Theology of the Body*, *op. cit.*, pp. 203–204. To anticipate a little, let me ask here, what would be the result of some disturbance in the state of the body vis-à-vis the relation of man and woman, the sacrament of the body, and the language of the body? Something that managed to "disincarnate" human beings, however temporarily? Were the body to become detachable, it would immediately assume the status of an aesthetic object.

121   Marshall McLuhan and Eric McLuhan (Toronto: University of Toronto Press, 1988).

122   Eric McLuhan and Wayne Constantineau, five-book series (Toronto: BPS Books, 2010–2015).

123   These transformations are detailed in the first part of *Laws of Media: The New Science*.

124   The poet Ezra Pound captured the artists' apparent foreknowledge of such conditions in his pithy declaration, "Artists are the antennae of the race." *ABC of Reading* (New York: New Directions, 1960), pp. 73 and 81.

125   From "What Dante Means to Me," in *To Criticize the Critic: Eight Essays on Literature and Education* (New York: Farrar, Straus & Giroux, 1965), p. 134.

126   From *The Western Canon: The Books and School of the Ages*,

by Harold Bloom (New York: Harcourt Brace & Company, 1994), p. 479.

127 *De Spiritualibus Creaturis (Disputed Questions on Spiritual Creatures)*, Art. I, *Respondeo*.

128 "The aspiration of our time for wholeness, empathy and depth of awareness is a natural adjunct of electric technology. The age of mechanical industry that preceded us found vehement assertion of private outlook the natural mode of expression. Every culture and every age has its favorite model of perception and knowledge that it is inclined to prescribe for everybody and everything. The mark of our time is its revulsion against imposed patterns. We are suddenly eager to have things and people declare their beings totally. There is a deep faith to be found in this new attitude—a faith that concerns the ultimate harmony of all being. Such is the faith in which this book has been written." Marshall McLuhan, *Understanding Media: The Extensions of Man* (New York: McGraw-Hill, 1964), Introduction.

129 *Ibid.*, Art. VIII, *Respondeo*. The quoted matter is from the third of his reasons.

130 An early example is "horseless carriage"; a recent one, "electronic book."

131 Joseph Cardinal Ratzinger, responding to an interview question. Joseph Cardinal Ratzinger, with Vittorio Messori, *The Ratzinger Report: An Exclusive Interview on the State of the Church*, tr. Salvator Attanasio and Graham Harrison (San Francisco: Ignatius Press, 1985), p. 73.

132 There are four ways to write: phonetic alphabets (of which there are fewer than a half dozen), syllabaries (which make up nearly all of the writing systems on earth), pictograms (such as Chinese characters), and ideograms (each

character represents an idea). Perhaps not surprisingly, the four stand in analogical ratio.
133 I.e., the *sensus communis* reconfigures around the new influence.
134 Maryanne Wolf, *Proust and the Squid: The Story and Science of the Reading Brain* (New York: HarperCollins, 2007), pp. 4–5.
135 Ellul, *Propaganda: The Formation of Men's Attitudes* (New York: Vintage Books, 1973), p. 162.
136 Ellul, *op. cit.*, p. 108.
137 David Booth, *Reading Doesn't Matter Anymore: Shattering the Myths of Literacy* (Markham, ON: Pembroke Publishers, 2006; Portland, ME: Stenhouse Publishers, 2006), p. 53.
138 www.youtube.com/watch?v=Jny1M1hI2jc
139 This is a brief outline: see *Laws of Media: The New Science* for a full treatment.
140 One reliable sign of obsolescence is a sudden proliferation of the old thing. Even while newspapers are disappearing, and publishing houses and the number of used-book stores dwindle, paradoxically we find ourselves awash in a spate of newly-minted "literacies." For example, we have cultural literacy, media literacy, television literacy, computer literacy, art literacy, etc., etc. New literacies are announced virtually daily. Appendix Four, *infra.*, presents a partial list of these forms. These little literacies have no relation whatever to alphabetic Literacy or to *littera* (letters). They do represent, on the other hand, a development in the direction of "reading" the contemporary world as a book.
141 *The Disappearance of Childhood*, p. 133.
142 Reports Diana West, in *The Death of the Grown-Up: How*

America's Arrested Development Is Bringing Down Western Civilization (New York: St. Martin's Press, 2007), p. 1: "More adults, ages eighteen to forty-nine, watch the Cartoon Network than watch CNN. Readers as old as twenty-five are buying 'young adult' fiction written expressly for teens. The average video gamester was eighteen in 1990; now he's going on thirty. And no wonder: the National Academy of Sciences has, in 2002, redefined adolescence as the period extending from the onset of puberty, around twelve, to age thirty." (The last fact is from Marcel Danesi, *Forever Young: The 'Teen-Aging' of Modern Culture* [Toronto: University of Toronto Press, 2003], pp. 104–105).

143 *Doom of Youth* (New York: Robert M. McBride and Co., 1932), p. 265.

144 Wyndham Lewis, *The Art of Being Ruled* (London: Chatto & Windus, 1926), p. 285.

145 Lasch, *The Minimal Self: Psychic Survival in Troubled Times* (New York and London: W. W. Norton, 1984), p. 164.

146 Wyndham Lewis, *The Enemy: A Review of Art and Literature*, Edited and Illustrated by Wyndham Lewis, No. 1 (January 1927, rpt., Santa Rosa, CA: Black Sparrow Press, 1994), pp. 75–76.

147 *Op. cit.*, p. 71.

148 Cf. Second Vatican Ecumenical Council, Constitution on the Sacred Liturgy, *Sacramentum Consilium*, 59.

149 *The Light of Faith—Lumen Fidei*, *op. cit.*, pp. 75–76.

150 Cf. *Man and Woman He Created Them: A Theology of the Body*, *op. cit.*, 36:5–37:6, 94:6–95b:2.

151 *Ibid.*, pp. 537–38.

152 *The Ratzinger Report*, *op. cit.*, p. 84.

153 *Ibid.* Note, this conversation took place thirty years ago. Consider the "advances" made since then in genetics and gene manipulation, to mention just one area.
154 *Ibid.*, p. 87.
155 *Man and Woman He Created Them: The Theology of the Body, op. cit.*, pp. 510–511.

RELIGION

DEAR PATIENT READER, I thank you for your willingness to accompany me thus far, and perhaps even farther; but this essay must end somewhere. There can be no proper end or resolution as matters are still developing at a furious rate in our cultures. The foregoing notes and observations have constantly been on the verge of bursting into new (and extensive) territory and have had to be reined in dozens of times. The following quotation, by John Paul II, is a case in point: while it does tie together a number of matters preceding and also to be found in the appendices, it opens doors for further (and essential) discussion.

> The body is not subject to the spirit as in the state of original innocence, but carries within itself a constant hotbed of resistance against the sprit and threatens in some way man's unity as a person, that is, the unity of the moral nature that plunges its roots firmly into the very constitution of the person. The concupiscence of the body is a specific threat to the structure of self-possession and self-dominion, through which the human person forms

itself. And it also constitutes a specific challenge for the person. In any case, *the man of concupiscence does not rule his own body in the same way, with the same simplicity and "naturalness" as the man of original innocence.* The structure of self-possession, which is essential for the person, is in some way shaken in him to its very foundations; he identifies himself anew with this structure in the degree to which he is continually ready to win it.[156]

Our "odyssey" began simply, with de Lubac's observation on the character of the anagogical experience. As I read those words, I was struck by the near identity of that experience and the experience of oral poetry in Greece before the alphabet appeared. I determined to write a note on the overlap. No sooner had I started the note when the subject of the *sensus communis* suggested itself; therewith the note expanded into an essay, but I expected that even then it would not take more than a dozen pages or so. It was not long before I realized that there is more than a single *sensus communis*, and at that moment this became a much-enlarged discussion. As I proceeded I discovered that there is yet a third *sensus communis* consisting of the three theological virtues. It is clear that this essay really ought to be a full book, or two books. What we have above is a sort of prologue or a set of notes to aid in beginning that longer, proper study. Now, my own training is in literature and in the study of media and cultures, not in theology; so I have confined myself to matters of sense and sensibility and experience; I have avoided entering into theological disputation, though the matters I have discussed here do indeed present a multitude of opportunities for theologians to exercise their wits.

I trust that my own contributions here will help clarify the dimensions of the challenges facing the Church and us in our time. Given the nature of those challenges, given particularly the disorientation stirred up by the (relatively) new state of bodiliness, an understanding of the *sensus communis* bids fair to provide an avenue for resolving at least some of the questions we face personally and culturally. For example, there has been no consideration of the impact of the traditional Latin Mass and that of the newer "dialogue Mass" and vernacular Mass vis-à-vis the *sensus communis* of the faithful, not to mention the celebrant.[157] Yet it is a commonplace that the newer forms inhibit private prayer and meditation during Mass while the Latin Mass encouraged them. The causes of these dislocations are not ideological but perceptual.

Elsewhere I have suggested the need for a specifically Catholic approach to the matter of communication. I think there is matter enough in these pages to suggest some lines upon which such an approach might be begun and conducted. Pope John Paul II's monumental *Male and Female He Created Them: A Theology of the Body* appeared against the *ground* of (in the context of) the many new disembodiments of the user of electric media: a complementary study is clearly, and urgently, indicated, i.e., a *Theology of the Bodiless*, for want of a better title.

Clearly, too, the present circumstances demand renewed and continuing emphasis on the theological virtues, and on understanding of and reception of the sacraments.

Let Henri de Lubac, who initiated this odyssey, have the last word:

It has been and still is indispensable, in opposition to the falsely supernatural illusions of an airy apostolate, as well as the pharisaism of the privileged, to insist upon the conditions about which it would be vain to preach the practice of Christian virtues to the masses. More profoundly, it is good to react against certain social structures which, being dehumanizing, are the natural enemies of any faith. But do not go thinking that faith and Christian virtues would flourish automatically in a society where these obstacles would have been removed. A living seed fructifies in the most unpromising ground, and, without sowing, the best soil will always be barren. The question of the seed will always remain the essential question. The religious problem, everywhere and always, is essentially a problem of the spiritual order. The deep-seated causes of dechristianization and the profound factors of rechristianization will always be of the spiritual order.[158]

Notes

156 *Man and Woman He Created Them: A Theology of the Body*, op. cit., p. 244.

157 That is, reconfiguration of the *sensus communis* under the influence of new media environments produced an unexpected hunger in the laity for group participation in the liturgy to replace the practice of private prayer and private meditation.

158 *Paradoxes of Faith* (San Francisco: Ignatius Press, 1987), pp. 69–70.

APPENDIX ONE

Aristotle's Media War[159]

A BASIC ASSUMPTION BEHIND any theory of communication is that communication entails change, that communication means effect. If there is no effect, if the audience does not change, there is no communication. The approach is rhetorical to the core.

Therefore, two questions need to be asked in order to specify Aristotle's—or anyone's—theory of communication: What is his intended audience? And what effect does he aim to produce on that audience?

Aristotle was not, like Plato, or Sophocles or Aeschylus, a playwright, so his audience was not the common man: it may fairly be said to be his students and colleagues at the academy. As to the second question, the effect he wished to achieve shows up clearly in what is taken to be his biggest contribution to logical thought. In the *De Anima*, Aristotle says that all of the people around him think in images. He takes it for granted that his audience does so, and it is not to his liking.

> Now for the thinking soul images take the place of direct perceptions; and when it asserts or denies that they are good or bad, it avoids or pursues them. hence the soul never thinks without a mental image.[160]

That is, he assumes this habit on the part of all or nearly all of his contemporaries, including his students and colleagues. He regards thinking in images not as a valuable faculty but rather as a *debility*, and that is why he never counts it among the main faculties of the soul. Thinking in images completely shortcuts abstract reasoning, which he was wont to encourage. Since abstract thinking was fundamental to logic and philosophy (Dialectic), Aristotle absolutely *had* to find some way to circumvent the pernicious habit of thinking in images. And he found it: the syllogism.

It is utterly impossible to syllogize in images: the syllogism forces the mind to think using words, to reason using the left hemisphere of the brain exclusively. But don't take my word for it. I've tried syllogizing in images, and I invite you to make the experiment yourself.

The syllogism ruptures the mimetic thrall in which the poets held their Greek hearers, the same spell against which Plato inveighed in *Republic* and elsewhere and which Eric Havelock and Jacques Lusseyran describe so eloquently. The old habit posed a mortal threat to the new enterprise of abstract reasoning. Plato, however, never went further; at least, there is no evidence of his attempting actually to circumvent image-based thinking. Perhaps this is understandable inasmuch as Plato's background included a spell as a street-corner mime. It took his pupil, Aristotle, to respond to the challenge.

Perhaps you, reader, can compress a few images into a semblance of a syllogism. If you haven't done so before now, try it. Try the following (or any other) syllogism: convert each line—major premise, minor premise, conclusion—into an image. Any syllogism at all will serve as a model. Here is the classic example:

> All men are mortal.
> Socrates is a man.
> Therefore, Socrates is mortal.

Right off, you find that the major premise (the first line) cannot be made a single image.

You might possibly imagine a picture of all men and women, but a real picture (would it be head-and-shoulders portraits only or full-body images?) of every human being on earth at this moment would be impossibly large, perhaps miles in width and miles in height. The same would have been true of a picture of all humans on earth in Aristotle's or in Socrates's time. But the oral man, the preliterate man, would find such a generalized image entirely too abstract for his imagination to construct. Barry Sanders has found much the same thing:

> Through his interviews, Luria could describe the broad outlines of thinking under the conditions of orality, but in the end he could learn little if anything of the native intelligence of his peasants. Any paper-test—indeed, most questions posed by a literate interviewer—strains the oral person to do something he or she seems unable to do, which we can call by any number of different

names—decontextualization, abstraction, disembedding, defining, describing, categorizing—things the average grammar school child does every night in homework assignments. For Luria's peasants, however, these concepts seemed foreign. They lived fully in their sensory world.[161] They saw no reason for removing themselves from it, and they had no tools for accomplishing that task. In the end, they refused to be pulled out of their immediate situation. Categorical terms held no practical use for them. "Tree" does not exist. But that tree stands over there; it provides shade and drops fruit. The pre-literate or non-literate remains deeply situated, and confronts experience by walking right up to it and grabbing hold of it.[162]

Well, just for argument's sake, allow that such an image might be constructed. So what would such an image "say"?

It actually would not "say" anything: it would simply depict all of humanity. *How* could anyone make it convey the notion of the statement "all men"? even supposing that you could overcome *that* difficulty, it is the copular verb that presents the real impossibility. A copula, as the word insists, is a joining device, a connection; images are not connected or sequential; they are whole entities: there is no right place to begin or to end. How can you adduce, then, in one and the same image, the notions "all men" and "mortal"? How for that matter can anyone invent an image of "mortal" or put a "mortal" spin on any image at all?

Very well, leave *that* aside for the moment and pass to the minor premise (the second line): "Socrates is a man." With this statement, you encounter the same problem. You might easily give an image of Socrates, but you cannot adjoin the copular "is," or the idea "a man," because "man" by itself is too abstract. How can you be specific (Socrates) and abstract (a man) at the same time and in the same image? Ask any painter. The trouble is, both major and minor premises of a syllogism are entirely abstract, lacking *ground*; images cannot work without some sort of *ground*.

And then you come to the conclusion (the third line). Even the bare idea "therefore" presents another impossibility. It is made of sequence. As before, you encounter sheer impossibility when you try to imagine a single image that will convey the abstract idea contained in the next three words, "Socrates is mortal." Can you assemble a series of images that make the same statement?

One simply cannot syllogize in images; it cannot be done.

Aristotle's syllogism constituted a real revolution in philosophy: it made abstract thinking much more precise in his time and for his audience. Dialectic—logic and philosophy—requires that you develop the capacity to think in words rather than in images. Images are entirely too illogical, too concrete; they do not provide any elbow room in the way of abstraction. As if by magic, Aristotle's syllogism defeats thinking in images, freeing the imagination to dance with ideas and cavort with words.

Our students today turn out to be pre-Aristotelian in their sensory lives. Almost every one of them, if questioned, will say that he or she normally thinks in images. They are right-brained[163] in their perceptual and cognitive bias. Teachers today therefore confront exactly the same problems with the mental lives of their students that Aristotle faced with his, with this difference: he was aware of the nature of the problem, and we for the most part are not. Further, Aristotle decided to take action and to modify his students' modes of thought; our teachers have evidently decided that the problem lies instead in their manner and technique of teaching. They figure that they must have the wrong theory.

In any event, articulating Aristotle's battle with image-based thought may go some distance to helping us solve a practical and growing problem in classrooms today. Aristotle was looking at the difference between the alphabet and the lingering power of the spoken word. Presently, we have print and the alphabet on the one hand, and the electronic word and electronic imageries on the other. Now, as then, it really is a matter of either-or.

In Aristotle's time, as in our own, traditional culture became the counter-culture. That always happens during a renaissance.

Notes

159 A version of these observations appeared in *Theories of Communication*, by Eric McLuhan and Marshall McLuhan (New York: Peter Lang, 2011), pp. 189–92.

160 *Aristotle: On the Soul, Parva Naturalia, On Breath*. Loeb Classical Library. Tr. W. S. Hett (Cambridge, MA: Harvard University Press; London: William Heinemann, 1957), III. vii; 481a.14-17, pp. 176, 177: Τῇ δὲ διανοητικῇ ψυχῇ τὰ φαντάσματα οἷον αἰσθήματα ὑπάρχει. ὅταν δὲ ἀγαθὸν ἢ ἀποφήσῃ, φεύγει ἢ διώκει. διὸ οὐδέποτε νοεῖ ἄνευ φαντάσματος ἡ ψυχή... (*ibid.*, p. 176.)

161 That is, they lived fully and completely in the here-and-now.

162 Barry Sanders, *A Is for Ox: The Collapse of Literacy and the Rise of Violence in an Electronic Age* (New York: Random House/Vintage Books, 1994), p. 32.

163 Ed. note (Andrew McLuhan): For a treatment of the human brain's two hemispheres relevant to this

discussion see "Culture and Communication: The Two Hemispheres" in *Laws of Media: The New Science* (Marshall and Eric McLuhan, University of Toronto Press, 1988).

APPENDIX TWO

Communication Arts in the Ancient World[164]

BEFORE WRITING APPEARED, THE ancients averred that all human wisdom is manifest in words. The lexicon of the tribe served as an encyclopedia of its knowledge, wisdom, and experience. The tribal poets tended this garden of eloquence.

The *logos* is therefore *the* medium of communication; as well, it supplied the cultural bond. But under the influence of alphabetic writing, the powerful mimetic *logos* of the pre-Socratics and the poets morphed into several new elements. Where before there was only speech, words now assumed three forms: the word in thought (silent), the written word, and the spoken word. The *logos* had been shattered. The fragments correspond to the three verbal modes of wisdom, as formulated by the Stoics:

The silent word is that of Dialectic, the *logos hendiathetos*.[165] It is the word in the mind, without speech. It is the skill of thinking in words and sentences. So Dialectic places its emphasis on mental processes, on logic and philosophy, and thinking aright.

The written word is that of Grammar, the *logos spermatikos*[166]—the *logos* as the seeds embedded in things, the seeds from which things grow and derive their essential nature. Consequently, Grammar places its emphasis on etymology and interpretation of both the written book and the Book of Nature. Grammar bridged the arts (four-level interpretation, four senses of Scripture) and sciences (four sciences: arithmetic, geometry, music, astronomy; and four causes: formal, efficient, material, final—all in analogical "proper proportion"). A grammarian regarded all of nature and every written text as his province. Grammar necessarily entailed encyclopedism.

The spoken word is that of rhetoric, the *logos prophorikos*.[167] So rhetoric emphasizes transformation—of audience—and decorum (and all five divisions: invention, disposition, elocution, memory, delivery). *Mimesis* survived in rhetoric as the agent of transforming audiences.

The Romans, having no single word for the Greek *logos*, used the hendiadys *ratio et oratio*, wisdom and eloquence. Based on this agreement, Cicero and Quintilian yoked oratory and encyclopedism, Eloquence and Grammar, Mercury and Philology[168] as the backbone of any serious cultural or intellectual enterprise.

Notes

164 An abbreviated version of this essay appeared in *Theories of Communication*, by Eric McLuhan and Marshall McLuhan (New York: Peter Lang, 2011), pp. 189–92.
165 λόγος ἐνδιάθετοσ.
166 λόγος σπερματικόσ.
167 λόγος προφορικόσ.

168 Yes, you'd best dig out your copy of Martianus Capella's *De Nuptiis Philologiae et Mercurii*. Note that the narrator is Dame Satire in person.

APPENDIX THREE

Paradoxes of the Mass Audience[169]

> Once out of nature I shall never take
> My bodily form from any natural thing,
> But such a form as Grecian goldsmiths make
> Of hammered gold and gold enamelling
> To keep a drowsy emperor awake;
> Or set upon a golden bough to sing
> To lords and ladies of Byzantium
> Of what is past, or passing, or to come.
> —W. B. Yeats, "Sailing to Byzantium"

OVER THE LAST FEW decades, we have immersed Western culture, indeed all the civilizations of the world, in a new *kind* of culture, a culture of disembodied hunters... of information. When information was simply content of an environment, the expert information-gatherer was master; now, with information our global environment, gathering is pointless. All of it is instantly available everywhere. Navigation and hunting are principal skills of nomads. Like their Paleolithic ancestors, our neo-nomads go, in electric form, where the game is to be found. The electric information environment takes the entire Neolithic age as its content and turns us all into nomadic hunters and huntresses.

The Church has always held the doctrine of individual souls and private salvation, which presupposes a ground of private identity and individual responsibility. But the Western world has latterly taken a turn in a different direction, due entirely to the effects of new media. Private individual identity no longer can be taken for granted in the high-participation world of the internet and interactive technologies. In this situation, even the idea of private salvation loses its meaning, relevance, and interest.

Elias Canetti reported that there are and always have been two modes of crowds, open crowds and closed crowds. He announces that the two modes of crowd are the same everywhere, regardless of culture or size or language or era.

The open crowd (the natural crowd) is everywhere spontaneous. It has a built-in need to grow, and it fears stagnating and shrinking.

> As soon as it exists at all, it wants to consist of more people: the urge to grow is the first and supreme attribute of the [open] crowd.
>
> It wants to seize everyone within reach; anything shaped like a human being can join it. The natural crowd is the open crowd; there are no limits whatever to its growth; it does not recognize houses, doors or locks and those who shut themselves in are suspect. "Open" is to be understood here in the fullest sense of the word; it means open

everywhere and in any direction. The open crowd exists so long as it grows; it disintegrates as soon as it stops growing.[170]

The open crowd is inherently unstable. The closed crowd, on the other hand, is stability itself:

> The closed crowd renounces growth and puts the stress on permanence. The first thing to be noticed about it is that it has a boundary. It established itself by accepting its limitation... the important thing is always the dense crowd in the closed room; those standing outside do not really belong. The boundary prevents disorderly increase, but it also makes it more difficult for the crowd to disperse and so postpones its dissolution.[171]

Broadly speaking, the West typifies the open crowd; the East, an uneasy mosaic of closed crowds. Any cult is a closed crowd. Both the open and closed forms are physical crowds, in physical space.

Today, at least a third of the world's population routinely participates in metaphysical crowds. You cannot understand this new situation by using any of the familiar techniques such as classification, or population-sampling or nose-counting or comparing locations, distances, etc. Only formal cause will reveal how environments operate.[172] Electric media profoundly challenge the very foundations of individual identity each time they absorb us into mass audiences. Neither our customary ground, private identity, nor basic tools like detachment and objectivity, can relate to participatory experience.

This new phenomenon, the mass audience, is invisible, composed as it is of *de facto* intelligences with no bodies. The average person daily uses interactive media from telephone to internet to satellite, at a cost: he and she are transformed into bits of electric information. This unconscious disembodiment contributes to the disorientation that people feel in the material world. Decades ago, the "digerati" began referring to the off-line experience as RL (real life), something comparatively exotic—or pedestrian. Physical life has been displaced by metaphysical life. Make no mistake: electric media translate us from physical entities into metaphysical entities for the first time in human existence.

On the telephone, the user is simultaneously here and there, no longer constrained by his physical body to be in one place at a time. The body remains where it was but is irrelevant to the new situation. At the same time, the interlocutor is simultaneously there, and here, also having left the body aside as irrelevant. *There is no movement from one place to another*, the way a letter moves about from sender to receiver, *just simultaneous existence in both "places" at once.*

Minus the physical body, the user of electric media can be in two or two dozen or two billion places simultaneously. On the radio, on television, the user is everywhere these media reach there and then. Once on the internet you are simultaneously everywhere the internet reaches, both actually and potentially.

The enabling environment for the mass audience is the totality of electric media present and operating, via broadcast, network, satellite, etc. So there is the radio crowd, the TV crowd, etc.—each a dialect, as it were, a particular mode of the mass.

The mass audience cannot have distant goals or directions or objectives. Those matters pertain to *incarnate* experience, to *becoming*, whereas the mass is involved rather with *being*—being in the now. Now, being is, of course, not an objective or a goal. With no outer physical body, the mass audience shifts its focus inward. This trope inward also appears disguised as narcissism. But it is the narcissism or the selfishness of one without a self, which is rather different from the selfishness that attends private individualism.

Online or on the air, minus your physical bodies, you put on the corporate body: you wear all mankind as your skin. Under these conditions, a merely private sensibility would be a huge liability.

The term "mass audience" was coined to denote broadcast-media crowds. *Sheer speed makes the mass, not size or numbers.* So we have the paradox that *all mass audiences regardless of composition are the same size*. Physical size and number characterize *incarnate* crowds.[173]

At electric speed, there is no to or fro: the user just manifests here *and* there, having left the body behind (somewhere or other). "There" might be the other side of the world or the other side of town, or both: it's all the same. "On the air" you can "be" in thousands or millions of places simultaneously.

Physical laws don't apply once you leave the physical body for metaphysical being: there is nothing on which to base them.

There is no human metaphysical sensus communis. Or is there?

The user of electric media has become information, an environmental image, exempt from natural law. Once out of nature…

Notes

169 Much of the material in this appendix is taken from a speech delivered at the Gregorian University in Rome, in 2008.

170 *Crowds and Power*, tr. Carol Stewart (London: Victor Gollancz, 1962; New York: Viking, 1963; New York: Penguin Books, 1973; rpt. Peregrine Books, 1987, *et seq.*, p. 17.

171 *Ibid.*

172 See "On Formal Cause," by Eric McLuhan, *Explorations in Media Ecology* 4 (nos. 3–4), 2005, pp. 181–210.

173 The laws of physics declare that any particle moving at the speed of light acquires zero size and infinite mass.

APPENDIX FOUR

Literacies

We have decapitated the Hydra
and in her place are springing up
hundreds of little baby literacies!

To communicate with Mars, converse with spirits,
To report the behavior of the sea monster,
Describe the horoscope, haruspicate or scry
Observe disease in signatures, evoke
Biography from the wrinkles of the palm
And tragedy from fingers; release omens
By sortilege, or tea leaves, riddle the inevitable
With playing cards, fiddle with pentagrams
Or barbituric acids, or dissect
The recurrent image into pre-conscious terrors—
To explore the womb, or tomb, or dreams; all these are usual
Pastimes and drugs, and features of the press:
And always will be, some of them especially
When there is distress of nations and perplexity.[174]

RATHER THAN BEGIN WITH definitions, let us take the poetic route and inventory the acknowledged "literacies" around us. In no particular order, then, we find:
- Augury [Ought we to haruspicate or scry?].
- Lip reading.
- Face reading.
- Body language.
- Symptomology—the body as book. For that matter, nearly all of the recognized -ologies would qualify as literacies. here are a few: anthropology, etymology, horology, physiology, demonology, martyrology, sexology, criminology, chronology, doxology, astrology, cardiology, biology, zoology, phrenology, ecology, geology, Assyriology, Egyptology, serology, osteology, Sinology, Scientology, topology, theology, hematology, sociology, virology, psychology, toxicology, neurology, climatology, tropology, primatology, typology, kinesiology, hydrology.
- The hunter—reads sign.
- The tracker—reads sign.
- The detective, the CSI—reads the scene.
- Cultural literacy—meaning, usually, how well-read is the candidate in basic facts and factoids concerning this or that culture? E. D. Hirsch went in search of the culture archetypes and found instead a heap of battered clichés. Basic to this topic, though, is encyclopedism.
- In a similar vein, *Religious Literacy* (title of a late-2007 book-club offering, subtitled *What Every*

American Needs to Know—And Doesn't) offers "the core tenets of the world's religions, along with a wealth of religious stories."
- Cultural anthropology—reads native and other cultures as texts.
- Reading an X-ray? Requires close observation, powers of discernment.
- Reading aloud as distinct from reading silently: they are sufficiently distinct as to merit recognition as separate literacies. That would make of speed-reading a third mode of literacy. Richard Lanham regards reading aloud and reading silently as each offering a distinct posture of the sensibilities and of the imagination. I.e., of the *sensus communis*.
- Truman Capote once dismissed another's prose with "that's not writing, that's typing": at a stroke he identified a different literacy—a style dictated by the typewriter. It introduced the nineteenth century to a range of new prose styles and experiences.
- "Word processing" then also identifies a literacy; certainly documents created thus, rather than, say, handwritten in ink on paper, have their own style and freedoms and constraints.
- E-literature today delights in exploring the farthest recesses of digital freedom, and is still in the sandbox stage—that of greatest creative experimentation.
- Here is a current suggestion, found on the internet: "In the war against "super bugs" like

MRSA, scientists are finding that the way to defeat them and any other bacteria may be by disrupting their communication. As this ScienCentral News video explains, decoding the language of bacteria might lead to powerful new antibiotics."

That suggestion opens the door to a number of additional literacies. Evidently alphabetic literacy has not been the only casualty of our new hunger for involvement. Numbers as well as letters work via detachment and abstraction. Therefore, we must include:

- Numeracy—which recently hit the headlines for a decade or so as various groups lamented its demise. In *Innumeracy*, J. A. Paulos observed:

    Quasi-mathematical questions arise naturally when one transcends one's self. How many? How long ago? How far away? How fast? Which is more likely? How do you integrate your projects with local, national, and international events? With historical, biological, geological, and astronomical time scales?
    People too firmly rooted to the center of their lives find such questions uncongenial at best, quite distasteful at worst. Numbers and "science" have appeal for these people only if they're tied to them personally... Getting such people interested in a numerical or scientific

fact for its own sake or because it's intriguing or beautiful is almost impossible.

Excessive concern with oneself makes it difficult to see this and thus can lead to depression as well as innumeracy.[175]

- "Media literacy," which in general parlance means having the skills necessary to recognize, evaluate, and apply the techniques of this or that medium. The emphasis is always on efficient cause, on cause-and-effect, because the focus is on content and application. The term rather vaguely subsumes a number of media and their respective literacies. So, for example, computer literacy or film literacy. Or any of the others:

- TV, radio, internet, or photographic literacies abound, but no one, interestingly, has proposed telephone or telegraph literacy. A very few media do not (yet) have an associated literacy, and they make a good study in themselves.

- Each of the arts has its own literacy as well as its own literature, and so: music literacy, and dance literacy, etc. There is also an overall arts literacy and literature.

- Precisely the same may be said of the sciences, with perhaps greater force than of the arts inasmuch as separations between the sciences are emphasized more than those between the arts.

- In the speculative column one might find decipherment as a candidate for inclusion as a literacy. Michael Ventris deciphered Linear B (a syllabary that preceded the alphabet) and opened thereby a window on the Greek Bronze Age. He made it possible to read the script for the first time. Champollion, similarly, deciphered Egyptian hieroglyphic and demotic using the Rosetta Stone and drew aside the curtains obscuring ancient Egypt's literature. And if one admits these as yet another subfamily of literacies, what is one to do with more professional codes and ciphers, and those who decode and decipher? Vignere? Playfair? Enigma? These are but the vestibule to a rich world (and lamentably one irrelevant to our designs).

All of the literacies discussed above, including the several media literacies, can without strain be subsumed under the heading **Literacies of the Arts and the Sciences**. This is to recognize that the hallowed separations between the arts, and those between the sciences, and those between the arts and the sciences, have in practice long ago dissolved. Whoever masters multiple literacies in order to function, at school or on the job, is engaged in obliterating those separations and exploiting the energies released when sciences or arts or both brush up against each other.

[Digital Storytelling] raises new aspects of language. The range of texts available to students spans not only literary genres and cultures but nonprint media forms as well. Students need to be able to "read" TV programming, digital stories, online discussions, and other kinds of media collages that consume much of the bandwidth in their tEcosystem [sic]... experiencing more contemporary works in new media form ideally situates [students] to be literate in the most useful, contemporary sense.[176]

Such versatility in compounding various media and sundry literacies characterizes the digital world. Once transmuted into software, anything and everything becomes malleable, fluid, interchangeable. The digital is a world of instant transformation, and now it is running at warp speed.

The whirlwind of new media in the last decade has brought a corresponding kaleidoscope of styles and forms of awareness. When change is relatively slow, the need for training awareness is not so pressing. But when major new media appear every three or four years, the need becomes a matter of survival. Each new medium is a new culture and each demands a new spin on identity; each takes root in one or another group in society, and as these flow in and out of each other the abrasive interfaces generate much violence. It is urgent that we begin to study all of the forms of knowing, now called literacies. Multimedia means simply compound literacies. As discourse shifts from page to screen and, more significantly to a networked environment, as discourse decentralizes, the established definitions and relations automatically undergo substantial change. The shift in our world view from individual to network holds the promise of a radical reconfiguration in culture. Notions of authority are being challenged with each rise in the beholder's share.

Every increase in participation decreases objectivity and detachment.

Naturally, every change in any of these areas brings a corresponding change to the inner harmony of the *sensus communis*.

Notes

174   T. S. Eliot, *Four Quartets*, "The Dry Salvages," ll. 184–97.
175   Ibid., pp. 81, 82.
176   Jason Ohler, *Digital Storytelling in the Classroom: New Media Pathways to Literacy, Learning and Creativity* (Thousand Oaks, CA: Corwin Press, 2008), pp. 46–47.

APPENDIX FIVE

Effects of the Discarnate

WOMEN'S LIB AND OUTLAWING of "discrimination" of all sorts based on body:

height, weight, shape or proportions, age(ism), gender (sexism), colour (racism)
new sexual freedom
legitimization of same-sex "parentage" of families
legitimization of same-sex marriage
legitimization of and social tolerance of prostitution
legitimization of lesbianism and homosexuality as merely lifestyle "choices"
destruction of childhood
disappearance of adulthood
disappearance of childhood (Neil Postman; Wyndham Lewis)
language of the body >> muted
body rendered as programmable, art form:
    tattoos, piercings
    drugs:

    mood-changing, uppers, downers
    psychopharmaceuticals (LSD, pot, XTC, cocaine,
        heroin, mushrooms, mescaline, etc.)
      weight reduction
      Viagra, etc.
      contraceptives, abortifacients
    surgery:
      liposuction
      reshaping: breast enlargement / reduction
      replacement of organs using other people's /
      animals', prosthetic limbs, organs
    sex-change operations
hedonism rampant, body is for kicks (recreational)
    sex reduced to aesthetics and athletics only;
      no sacramentality
      no responsibility
    sex toys and stimulants
    abortion as a right, a choice;
    abortion socially / legally accepted

Virtually everything in the last group is the subject of constant propaganda, even still.

In general, there is a pretty consistent pattern to the technological and chemical reformation of the body (experience and perception) and its relation to the *sensus communis* and to the soul.

This new situation results in a new culture of the body, the secularization of the body. What more dramatic evidence of this new sense of the body can one cite than the explosion of and legitimization (and toleration, if not acceptance) of pornography?

Note the close relation between the popularity of porn and the refusal to mature: porn serves as an accessory for oldsters trapped in prepubescence? It does perpetuate that adolescent angst.

"No individual identity" means the experience of private responsibility has been undermined >> diminish the personal perceived need for penance. We need no-fault sin, dammit! We have made a beginning...

>No-fault divorce
>No-fault auto insurance

In *The Ratzinger Report*, Cardinal Ratzinger expanded on his observation that motherhood and sexuality have been wrenched apart with disastrous results.

In his view we will atone already in our day for the "consequences of a sexuality which is no longer linked to motherhood and to procreation. It logically follows from this that every form of sexuality is equivalent and therefore of equal worth." "It is certainly not a matter," he specifies, "of establishing or recommending a retrograde moralism, but one of lucidly drawing the consequences from the premises: it is, in fact, logical that pleasure, the *libido* of the individual, become the only possible reference of sex. No longer having an objective reason to justify it, sex seeks the subjective reason in the gratification of the desire, in the most 'satisfying' answer for the individual, to the instincts no longer subject to rational restraints. Everyone is free to give to his personal *libido* the content considered suitable for himself."

He continues: "hence, it naturally follows that all forms of sexual gratification are transformed into the 'rights' of the individual. Thus, to cite an especially current example, homosexuality becomes an inalienable right. (Given the aforementioned premises, how can one deny it?) On the contrary, its full recognition appears to be an aspect of human liberation."

There are, however, other consequences of "this uprooting of the human person in the depth of his nature." Ratzinger elaborates: "Fecundity separated from marriage based on a lifelong fidelity turns from being a *blessing* (as it was understood in every culture) into its opposite: that is to say a threat to the free development of the 'individual's right to happiness.' Thus abortion, institutionalized, free and socially guaranteed becomes another 'right,' another form of 'liberation.'"[177]

Notes

These remarks date from 1985, just before the explosion of pornography on the internet.

See also Appendix Eight, below, on artificial intelligence initiatives.

177 *The Ratzinger Report, op. cit.*, pp. 85–86.

APPENDIX SIX

The Blindfold Exercise

SOME FORTY YEARS AGO, I took a dozen or so art students to a retreat in central Ontario (a place called Innisfree, nestled in the woods) for a three-day weekend exercise in training of perception. They were all young, some still in, some just out of, their teens. I wanted to use a Lusseyran-like experience to help them discover and learn to play with senses other than sight. One of the participants was a young lady who had been completely blind since birth. Her role was to "keep the group honest," to expose any fakery or dishonesty by me or by any of the students. They were playing at being blind; she was not playing at it as they were. She was wonderful and had a lively sense of humour.

The students were asked to arrive at the retreat blindfolded (so that they would not have any preconceptions as to arrangements there), and to remain blindfolded as long as they could do so. There was no compulsion to keep the blindfold on: anyone could "drop out" at any time. Nearly all of them stayed the course. No concessions were made to their "blindness." For example, everyone assisted with meal preparation and cleanup.

They frequently gathered during the days to discuss their experiences and to listen to music and recordings of poets reading their work. I also read to them from, among other things, Lusseyran's biography *And There Was Light*.

As it was winter, shortly after they arrived we all went outside for a frolic in the snow (there was about ten inches on the ground), which soon turned into a snowball fight. Naturally, I became the target of preference. The curious thing is that after a few minutes nearly every snowball they threw at me connected: they became near-infallible.

All of them reported unusually acute awareness of large natural features, such as trees. Before the exercise ended, of the dozen, two or three "recovered their sight," Lusseyran-style, while blindfolded. This sight was not focused ahead of them as with ocular vision, but covered a 360-degree circle with them at the centre, rather as hearing works. I emphasize that these were ordinary students.

> There were blindfolded students who played tag with each other among the trees, chasing each other full tilt and avoiding every obstacle seemingly automatically. Some tried to "reason" against their sensory "intuition," and hearing their quarry cut right or left, attempted to cut a diagonal path to catch them. Wham, head first they hit the tree the quarry had avoided. And at the moment of impact these students experienced an instantaneous impression of the surrounding landscape in all directions, including trees and people, embedded in a red flash not unlike what remains on the retina after looking at a bright light.
>
> When it came time to remove the blindfolds,

everyone had the same experience: the world was painfully bright, flat, and abstract. It took several minutes for vision to sort the patterns of light and shadow into their customary depth.

At the end of the experiment, several students climbed trees before removing their blindfolds. Without perspective on height, they climbed thirty, even forty feet off the ground. They removed their blindfolds high in the tree. Two of them almost immediately decided to race down to the ground. They did not quickly descend a ladder of branches. With the tactile senses fully engaged they dropped out of the tree like stones, hands grasping at branches only long enough to control their descent. They both arrived on the ground safely in a heap, laughing with delight.[178]

After they returned home, those who had pets reported that they were virtually assaulted by the pets: the dogs or cats would simply not leave them alone; they were extremely attentive and affectionate—a condition that persisted for some days.

The following remarks were sent me by one of the participants (Peter S.), one of the men who climbed a tree before removing his blindfold. I present them separately since they are so detailed and so personal.

The Blindfold Experiments

In the early 1970s I studied at Fanshawe College in the new program Creative Electronics. Among the many interesting instructors we had was Eric McLuhan, son of Marshall.

Eric proposed a visual deprivation experience which we called the "Blindfold Experiments." The intent of the experiment was to see how people might adapt when they lose their sight.

I must admit I had concerns about my ability to function without sight, believing that I would be severely handicapped.

All of those participating in the experiment were in the Creative Electronics program which was designed for people planning a career in the music industry, many being musicians and all interested in music. We built a recording studio in the first year of the program and participated in many recording sessions, training our hearing to note subtle variations in sound. To this day I hear many background sounds which others do not. The experiment would, in part, test this skill.

Prior to the experiment we met Scout, a young blind woman who explained how she functioned in life without sight. She was very organized and independent and after meeting her I decided it might not be as limiting as I originally thought.

We were advised that we would be staying at a monastery for a weekend.[179] So we would have no visual clues, we were blindfolded before we arrived and were to remain blindfolded for the whole weekend, learning about the monastery and daily functions while deprived of sight. My preconceived ideas of what a monastery would be like were to be proved wrong.

Entering the monastery, I was dependent upon tactile and auditory senses to explore the building. While expecting to collide with objects in the house, I found that I could easily detect walls and larger objects by the change in sound. As I got closer to walls the reverb time for ambient sound would become shorter and I could "see" the wall.

During the weekend I started to develop a concept of the layout of the monastery. It was based on the sound of the rooms, the feel of the floors and touching the walls. All the walls felt the same as they were drywall so it was sound that distinguished the different rooms. The bedrooms sounded small, the living room sounded larger and there was an open walkway on the second floor above the kitchen. The kitchen sounded very large with the upper walkway as you could hear and talk to people moving above. I had an auditory sense of the place but I couldn't put it all together until we removed our blindfolds on the last day. It is amazing how different your perception is between audio and visual sources.

I learned some surprising things in the kitchen. I was afraid of the stove, convinced that cooking would be dangerous as I would burn myself. Actually, fingers are very sensitive to heat and can easily detect sources of heat and the location of hot objects. Quite by accident I found that you could touch the inside bottom of a pan on the stove and not burn yourself. Without sight, by using a gentle touch in the kitchen you can sense the heat before you come in contact with an object.

We were at the monastery in the autumn. Surrounded by woods filled with hardwood trees, the grounds were great for walks or playing games.

We started exploring the woods, finding we could hear the trees and avoid them while walking. Howie and Dean started playing tag which I thought would end in disaster. However Dean found that he did not collide with trees as long as he was having fun playing tag. When he started to get devious and try to deceive Howie he kept colliding with trees.

When I touched trees I could sense where neighbouring trees were located and walk to them. We had a person who was not blindfolded (Eric) who was watching and he said I could do this accurately every time I touched a tree. I'm sure the trees were communicating with each other through their roots. I still find this amazing. I have recently seen research which shows that trees can detect baby trees growing from their own seeds and then alter their root system to help their babies.

It has been many years since the Blindfold Experiments but I have benefitted from the skills I learned. I often walked through the house with the lights off and know I can navigate safely. I can pick up a piece of clothing and tell by feel what it is and how to put it on. While these skills are useful, they were never acute enough to detect Barbie shoes on the floor in the dark, often resulting in injury. I stopped walking in dark while my girls were young.

And here are some reminiscences of those Blindfold Exercises 1973 / 1974; selected passages from a journal by Dean M., one of the participants.

Laff in the Dark

The Blindfold Experiments as they came to be called consisted of a group of media students spending a three-day weekend blindfolded. This was done at a rural retreat, a wooded monastery that made itself available for church and educational groups. In addition to a couple of sighted monitors (who were only to interfere in cases of safety or of extreme difficulty and to read selected material aloud (especially matter by Lusseyran, and Marshall McLuhan)). Also in attendance was an accomplished blind young lady, nicknamed "Scout." She would help us explore a world without sight.

While I was excited by the prospect of the exercise, I also had some apprehension. After all, as an aspiring graphic artist, my training had been strictly visual. On the other hand most of my classmates were musicians. I wasn't sure I wouldn't be setting myself up for a weekend of frustration. I was beginning to understand the actual difference between "auditory space" (the ear) and "acoustic space" (all senses) as defined by McLuhan and described in detail by Lusseyran. The prior classroom readings from *And There Was Light* had prepared me objectively, but I was still secretly filled with trepidation. I dabbled in music, and certainly consumed enormous amounts of it in the form of record albums and concert attendance. But music had always been my inspiration, not my area of any adeptness. At the time I was a cartoonist with lofty if not pretentious ambitions in the realm of visual storytelling.

Nevertheless, the adventurous nature of what was being proposed was irresistible. It had the appeal of dealing with unexplored perceptions. Then there was the camaraderie of the group and even the prospect of enlightenment of some kind.

Lights Out

Despite our preparations with extended readings and discussion of Lusseyran, old habits died hard for me.

After orientation, upon being blindfolded two things occurred to me. One was that, after a while, the sense of self-imposed darkness was different from struggling to navigate a world of little or no visibility—where despite the lack of information one still strains to use one's vision and still regards the other senses as almost ornamental, or at least subordinate. This was different. I tried to use sound, smell and touch for vision to navigate what, in my mind, was still a visually "pictured" space. In fact I spent a long time creating a mental diagrammatic map. When

I became lost or disoriented, I would mentally deconstruct the map and reassemble it correctly. After a time I could rotate my model. But the level of concentration needed was exhausting and frustrating. As time went on the map became less and less useful. It required constantly translating audio/tactile information into imagined visual symbols. It was a cumbersome process and eventually abandoned.

I was convinced that I was going to be able somehow to train my other senses to be extra sensitive—or at least that I would be more aware of them. That I would master new skills to *replace* vision. That I might hear and interpret people's heartbeats. That I might echolocate like a bat. These skills, to the degree that they emerged at all, were subliminal. I was a bit disappointed. And I realized how much our eyes gave us the power to anticipate the dimensions of what we would encounter in a very specific way.

Blindfolded, these encounters were abrupt and sometimes painful. This was because I was still acting as if I was anticipating my encounters at the same speed. I had to slow down. Not so much for safety (though that was a consideration) as to encounter things in a gentler manner. I remembered in the past noticing how blind folks' movements, however slow and halting, seemed graceful—and thinking this was some sort of Zen they shared. Now I knew it was a practical way of "meeting" things. There was a warmth, even a softness, to even the hardest surfaces.

Sometime (after a nap, I think) on the second day the visual darkness had lifted. There was no longer the sense of being in a darkened room. No blackness. I came to think that that sensation was much like the reverberation of the final chord of a piece of music. A kind of echo in that visual interval. The next day I wasn't missing the visual sense as much (and filling the void with darkness that comes with the sudden lack of light) because I was no longer expecting it.

And so much of my mobility had become a tactile process, rather than a mechanical transition from one point to another. I began to think that it was more like swimming. Going through the environment as opposed to simply connecting origins to destinations. Maybe it was Zen after all.

Day to Day

In the course of each day we had our chores and ablutions to perform. It was interesting, discovering ways to accomplish these tasks using other senses. Filling a glass of water, for instance; it was easy enough to stick your finger in as you were pouring. But that seemed sloppy and unnecessary. Listening to a mini-Doppler effect, feeling the weight change seemed more elegant.

Preparing meals was challenging. Especially cooking. And though our sighted companions not only monitored us but helped when we became overly frustrated, nevertheless we were successful for the most part. I'm convinced that with more time we could've truly mastered blind cookery.

We went about our retreat as normally as possible. Our monitors watched and even challenged us to see what we were experiencing. I frequently could tell if someone was in the room, standing silent, motionless—waiting to be sensed. I could sometimes tell if someone was present and could hear him move if he quietly waved or gestured.

The Great Outdoors

A big part of the day was devoted to wandering. When we got adventurous we went outside and met the outdoors in a brand new way.

Playing games was a big part of it. Someone devised a game of catch, where a sighted person would throw a beach ball and on cue the blind catcher would shout something and echolocate the ball in mid-flight. Some became very adept at it.

Another was a game of tag, or "blind man's bluff,'" where the blindfolded would try to catch a sighted (and often mischievous) person. The faster the game was played the easier I found it to pursue and catch my quarry. Obviously it was acoustic signals that were at work here (breathing, clothes rustling, twigs and grass underfoot), but there was also a level of intuition that came into play when the sighted person froze and went to lengths to be undetectable. On one occasion we moved the game to a nearby field, so that we might be able to cover more distance. The field was chosen because it contained few obstacles and only a single tree in one corner. Oddly, almost every blindfolded person either encountered or slammed into the tree they had been warned about.

As time went on, people began spending time with the trees surrounding the retreat. Olaf, I think, showed us how to meet the trees, by hugging or caressing them. It seems laughable, but they gave a feeling of warmth and solidity that seemed almost spiritual. And there were various vibrations from within the building to the distant highway.

We spent a lot of time outside, whether it was playing games, wandering or just listening to the silence. It was surprising to me, how noisy, in this state, was the peacefulness of the country retreat. We would describe the sound to one another, trying to identify and find the significance of each. One night in particular, with the help of Scout, we tried and were reasonably successful in locating the full moon in the night sky. Whether we were picking up on the heat of the moonlight, the gravitational pull or some other subliminal cue entirely, it's difficult to say. But it seemed to work for some of us.

That's Entertainment

In the evening we would have discussion group wherein we would discuss what we had found, where we had failed and what our unexpected victories of the day had been. During these powwows Eric would often read to us. Usually it was passages from *And There Was Light*, or *Take Today* or *Oh, What a Blow That Phantom Gave Me*. The discussions that followed were quite illuminating, if you'll pardon the expression. One expected treat was his resonant voice reading from T. S. Eliot or Joyce's *Finnegans Wake*. The language took on a new dimension. It was as if the acoustics of the words read aloud revealed a more profound significance. More levels of meaning.

We had brought along a selection of music for the weekend, in the form of records. Most of the students had some background, if not professional aspirations, in the medium of recorded music, so it was surprising to me that most of us lost interest in listening to our favorite rock music in favor of Steve Reich or Gregorian Chants. Perhaps it was the mantra-like textures or the hypnotic acoustic structures. The rock music seemed very private somehow. Appealing to individual tastes, whereas the other appealed to the group as a shared audio/tactile experience.

Afterwards

When the day came to remove the blindfolds, we did it as a group, in a circle facing one another. As we took them off we kept our eyes closed, opening them on the count of three. It was overwhelming. People were elated, beaming, grinning from ear to ear. Certainly part of it was relief. Part of it was the amount of information rushing in. But there was something else. I think it was that, for a short time after, all our senses were in a highly receptive mode. We hadn't yet readjusted to visual domination. It was a kind of sudden intoxication. We went from room to room, from tree to tree, to identify with our eyes, if we could, the landmarks of our sightless world. Sometimes it was obvious. Other times it was startling how unfamiliar they looked. These were things that we had become intimate with by virtue of touch, smell and sound.

At the time I felt bad that Scout couldn't share this part of the exhilaration. But, as she told me later, she was not only at peace with it, but seemed to enjoy it both vicariously and viscerally.

In the weeks that followed the group would meet occasionally to discuss the aftermath of the Blindfold Experiment in their lives. Many had developed a taste for the poetry we had been read and the music we had listened to. That was to be expected. But some musicians reported being more in touch with their music, their instruments. Better performers. Many of us occasionally put on the blindfolds to relive/restore the sensations we experienced. My appreciation for cubist and primitive art went from being academic to practical, as if I truly understood (partly, anyway) the tactile, multi-dimensional worlds these forms portrayed. Some of our relationships became more intimate.

The experience was a life-changer for me on many levels. At the time it was a kind of perceptual funhouse. A world of new sensibilities—right at my own fingertips. In my own mind. After forty years, I'm probably due for another visit.

Addendum

I remember that once I stopped "picturing" things in my mind's eye, navigation—even basic manipulation of objects—became so much easier. It was exhausting to visualize everything that couldn't be seen, and then keeping track of all those images without any optical cues. The mind also fooled around with these images during sleep and near-sleep, to the point that sometimes the distortions were hard to distinguish from the "legit" visual models. I abandoned this whole effort—almost without knowing it—sometime during day two. I recall some participants saying that it was hard to cease this practice. Others gave up, and saw that as a failure in acquiring the skills that allow them to replace their vision. As if visual memory and imagination were to somehow become prosthetic eyes. I was surprised, with all the emphasis on my visual education,[180] that I was able to let go of this dimension at all. But once I was working with the environment in terms of the actual way that I was experiencing it, instead of how I imagined it must appear, the exercise become much easier. For one thing, structure changed. The unexpected—the unanticipated—didn't frustrate me as much. In fact, it was often the source of delight.

Notes
178 Personal correspondence from Howard W., one of the participants.

179 We performed two experiments, one group convened at Innisfree (mentioned above), and a second group, a few months later, at a nearby monastery. Both groups were of students in the same course.

180 Ed. note: the writer is an accomplished graphic artist.

APPENDIX SEVEN

A Catholic Theory of Communication[181]

ONLY TWO KINDS OF theory of communication are possible: sequential and simultaneous.

We in the West have used one theory for hundreds of years now; it served our needs quite well until electricity arrived and changed the ground rules.

Electric media to all intents and purposes operate instantaneously. The user is simultaneously here and there: you are there; they are here. In effect. At electric speeds, there is no movement; there is just presence. So the old theory, which was construed as movement of goods or information from place to place in chronological time, is not attuned to the new situation. We need a theory of communication that takes the new simultaneity into account and that sets aside all consideration of transportation.

Only one model of communication underlies all Western theories of media and of communication: the Shannon-Weaver model. It imagines a medium as a pipeline for moving hardware content or messages from place to place. It posits that in a successful communication, what was received matches exactly what was loaded into the pipeline by the sender:

Source > Message > Channel > Receiver

"Noise" from outside the pipeline surrounds and interpenetrates every aspect of the model. "Noise" means everything that is *not* the message, everything that the Source did not intend to send to the Receiver, but which the Receiver gets in spite of all attempts to suppress, avoid, and evade it. "Noise" would include all the unintended side effects of the medium.

Weaver interprets:

> The *information source* selects a desired *message* out of a set of possible messages... The selected message may consist of written or spoken words, or of pictures, music, etc.
>
> The *transmitter* changes this message into the *signal* which is actually sent over the *communication channel* from the transmitter to the *receiver*. In the case of telephony, the channel is a wire, the signal a varying electrical current on this wire; the transmitter is the site of devices (telephone transmitter, etc.) which change the sound pressure of the voice into the varying electrical current... In oral speech, the information source is the brain, the transmitter is the voice mechanism producing the varying sound pressure (the signal) which is transmitted through the air (the channel). In radio, the channel is simply space (or the aether, if anyone still prefers that antiquated and misleading word),

and the signal is the electromagnetic wave which is transmitted.

The *receiver* is a sort of inverse transmitter, changing the transmitted signal back into a message, and handing this message on to the destination... In the process of being transmitted, it is unfortunately characteristic that certain things are added to the signal which were not intended by the information source. These unwanted additions may be distortions of sound (in telephony, for example) or static (in radio), or distortions in shape or shading of picture (television), or errors in transmission (telegraphy or facsimile), etc. All of these changes in the transmitted signal are called noise.[182]

Claude Shannon: "The fundamental problem of communication is that of reproducing at one point either exactly or approximately a message selected at another point."[183] Actually, the multiplicity of side effects of any communication system forms an entire environment of interfacings, a subculture which accompanies the central "service" or channel of communication.

This Shannon-Weaver model of communication is the foundation under every model of the communication process and theory of communication in the civilized world. It focuses on moving packets of things or ideas from one place to another, from one person to another in sequential time. It is utterly unsuited to dealing with modern conditions, "modern" meaning since the invention of the telegraph in the mid-nineteenth century. Events in the electric world—our world today—are characterized by simultaneity and instant transformation, not gradual or sequential change. Any theory of communication that enables us to come to grips with modern conditions must begin with, be founded on, this fact of transformation.

The Other Path

A *transformation* theory, by contrast, is irrational. Quite simply, someone or something must change: communication is present when the audience changes. If there is no change, there has been no communication.

Communicating at electric speeds, there is no movement of information of idea from place to place or from person to person. Such things are simply simultaneously present everywhere at once. If you will, the "message" does not move from here to there; it is the sender that is sent. The audience ("receiver") performs a complementary maneuver and is suddenly everywhere at the same time. Both parties are simply, and suddenly, present everywhere.

On the air or on the telephone, the parties are simultaneously in two or more—maybe MANY more—places simultaneously. For the mass audience, there is no movement to or from, just simultaneity of being. This is a new experience of being, this separation from the body and its constraints. The new media, then, are not manifestations of physical communication so much as of *meta*physical communication. They entail the transformation of the users. The old body is still present, but irrelevant to the reality of the new situation. The body and its limitations are no longer deciding factors in human experience; the electric process has bypassed them all.

The Catholic Church has always accepted transformation at every level of communication. We believe in miracles, which are sudden transformations. We believe in sainthood. We believe in redemption: sudden transformation. We have developed our understanding of transformation over two thousand years, so we are in a grand position to provide the world with a working explanation of communication as instantaneous and transformative.

The Sacraments

The Catholic Church has traditionally devoted a large section of orthodox theology to this second method of communication: sacramental theology.

Each of the seven sacraments is a technology of communication in every real and tangible sense.

Each sacrament works by participation.

And each sacrament instantly transforms the participant. Some of the sacraments also make permanent and indelible marks on the soul of the participant. That is, the transformation is permanent.

Each sacrament is a *logos* of the Holy Spirit, a transforming *logos*. Pope John Paul II declared that, "as a sacrament of the Church, [marriage] is also a word of the Spirit exhorting man and woman to shape their whole life together by drawing strength from the mystery of the 'redemption of the body'" (*Male and Female He Created Them: A Theology of Body*, p. 522). The transforming logos has been a feature of communications studies for the last forty to fifty years. Eric Havelock discussed it at length in *Preface to Plato* as a fundamental mode of communication in the pre-alphabetic world.

The **medium of operation** of each sacrament is grace: sacramental graces and sanctifying grace. Speaking of media, recall that one of Our Lady's titles is "Mediatrix of all Graces"[184]: all graces that flow from heaven to earth flow through the medium of Our Lady.

- Baptism marks the soul for eternity and is irrevocable.

- Confirmation marks the soul for eternity, and is irrevocable.

- Marriage, once contracted, is for life and irrevocable.

- Holy Orders, too, is permanent and irrevocable.

- Penance cleanses the soul.

- Eucharist. The soul of communication: mystical communion itself.

There is an economy or ecology of the sacraments. We are given seven sacraments, not five or six, or eight or nine. Each one of the seven sacraments is absolutely necessary. Not one is superfluous; not one is lacking, to be revealed or given to us at some future time.[185] Seven it is. Every sacrament entails a change, a transformation of the user.

In the same book, John Paul calls marriage "the primordial sacrament," observing:

> Thus, as the primordial sacrament, marriage is assumed and inserted into the integral structure

of the new sacramental economy, which has arisen from redemption *in the form, I would say, of a "prototype."* It is assumed and inserted, as it were, from its very basis. In the dialogue with the Pharisees (Mt. 19:3-9), Christ Himself confirms first of all its existence. If we reflect deeply on this dimension, we have to conclude that all the sacraments of the New Covenant find their prototype in some way in marriage as the primordial sacrament.

[In the same dialogue, he continues,] Christ not only confirms the existence of marriage instituted from the "beginning" by the Creator, but He declares also that it is an integral part of the new sacramental economy, of the new order of salvific "signs" that draws its origin from the sacrament of redemption, just as the original economy emerged from the sacrament of creation...

It is significant that the sacraments presume and depend on the reality of the body; the new discarnate circumstances provided by mass media therefore may well pose a threat to the sacramental system of the Church. Certainly, the meaning of an incarnate Church to a discarnate laity differs deeply from what it meant before the advent of mass media. We ignore these matters at our peril.

The operation of grace in the soul is instantaneous, not gradual: it is a sudden transformation. For example, St. Thomas Aquinas explains how the soul passes from a state of sin to a state of grace as follows:

> The succession of opposites in the same subject must be looked at differently in the things that are subject to time and in those that are above time. For in those that are in time, there is no last instant in which the previous form inheres in the subject; and this for the reason, that in time we are not to consider one instant as immediately preceding another instant, since neither do instants succeed each other immediately in time, nor points in a line... But time is terminated by an instant. Hence in the whole of the previous time wherein anything is moving towards its form, it is under the opposite form; but in the last instant of this time, which is the first instant of the subsequent time, it has the form which is the term of the movement.[186]

The change of state entails an instantaneous transformation.

Every one of the sacraments is of heavenly origin: none is a merely human institution. Pope John Paul II remarks that marriage is the first of the sacraments, having been given to humanity in the Garden of Eden. Others were given to us directly by Our Lord (Penance, Eucharist). Pope John Paul also pointed out, in *Crossing the Threshold of Hope* (p. 130) that "all the sacraments are the action of Christ, the action of God in Christ."

Christ is THE medium: He administers each of the sacraments; it is He through whom all things were made; it is through Him alone that each of us may come to the Father. This fact ought to form a central element of any Christian theory of communication. The Church is the medium of salvation, and its medium is the Mystical Body.

Some sacraments are available to all people, inside as well as outside the Catholic Church: Marriage, Baptism.

Some of the sacraments are available only inside the Catholic Church: Holy Orders, Eucharist. For these, you might say, the Church is the medium of transmission.

In another sense, the main medium through which all of the sacraments operate is the medium of grace, sanctifying grace, sacramental grace. The study of graces and decorum will form a main concern of any Catholic theory of communication.

The electric age, the age of electric media and simultaneous and discarnate transformation of users and mass audiences, demands that we set aside transportation approaches to understanding media and understanding communication. They are irrelevant to the new circumstances, being linear and sequential. But they are still the only game in town, as it were; they are still the only kinds of "communication" that the world recognizes as valid approaches to the matter.

Yet the Church has for centuries nurtured and husbanded and actively used transformation as its approach to communication. "To communicate" does after all mean to take communion, to receive the Eucharist. And there is another form of communicating, of communion, of community that gives a basis for any Catholic theory of communication: simultaneity and transformation characterize not only the working of the sacraments but also our sense of Tradition and of the Communion of the Saints—yet another aspect of Catholic communication. The time is overdue to bring together the scattered fragments of our Catholic understanding of the communicative process, and to state the Catholic theory of communication. The world is in turmoil, is confused. For the traditional theory has no power to explain the present. The consequent state of confusion and disharmony surely presents the Father of Lies with great opportunities.

A Catholic Communications Degree

With a clear sense of communication as a transformative process, it would be natural as a next step to mount a Catholic communications degree program.

Students who wish to pursue a Catholic degree in communication will need to have a good grounding in both of the two books, both Scripture and Nature. Knowledge of Scripture will require that they actually read the Scriptures and a fair bit of commentary, certainly the great ones: Augustine, Jerome, Aquinas, Bonaventure, and others. They will have to know, too, the wellsprings of the tradition in Homer and Hesiod and the commentators, plus Greek and Roman literature, Varro, Cicero, Quintilian, Priscian, and Donatus, and so forward through literature and poetics at least as far as the twentieth century. One effect of this program ought to be to restore the unity of the arts and sciences, sundered since Descartes.

A Catholic degree in communication would not just consist of a dozen or so courses in journalism, radio and TV products and production, "new media" and theories, and some general arts requirements. It would entail a measure of that, yes, but not as much as is usually the case. It would, however, require a pretty good grounding in the Tradition, not as sterile history but as active resource bank.

Such a degree would mean that the students would have been schooled in the Catholic media. One such medium, that of the transmission of God's revelation to us, is the twin sources, Scripture and Tradition. This would mean having not just read about but having read the Fathers (well, some of them; there's quite a lot of it for just four years) and working with their ideas. A side effect should be to arm the students with orthodoxy against some of the heresy floating around. Heresy, too, can be profitably studied in media terms. Study of Scripture and Tradition means learning to read multiple texts, a skill set that dovetails well with the modern approach to multiple literacies in media education. Needless to say, the "multiple literacies" approach has a long and distinguished history in the area of reading the Book of Nature.

I invite you to keep these matters in mind during your deliberations here concerning the present and the future of liberal studies and our mission as educators. The several areas of focus, of beauty, and good, and truth, invite contemplation of, respectively, all forms of communication; environmental, technological, and cultural development; and critical thought. These three roads run right through the matters I have attempted to outline in the foregoing remarks.

Thank you.

Notes

181 Text of a speech delivered at the Pontifica Universita Lateranense in Rome, on the occasion of the VIIIth International Symposium of University Professors, June 23–25, 2011.

182 Claude Elwood Shannon and Warren Weaver, *The Mathematical Theory of Communication* (Champaign: University of Illinois Press, 1963), pp. 7–8.

183 *Ibid.*, p. 32.

184 In notes to the Mass for May 31, the *Saint Andrew Daily Missal* offers the following: "The will of God is that we

should have everything through Mary," says St. Bernard. The Father has sent us His Son, but His will was to make His coming depend upon the Fiat of the Virgin, which He commanded the angel Gabriel to solicit on the day of the Annunciation.

The Father and the Son send us the Holy Ghost, but it is through Mary that He comes down to men. On the day of the Pentecost, according to an ancient Tradition, the heavenly fire which descended on the Cenacle first rested on Mary, and then on the apostles. This is a figure of what happens every day in the Church where the Holy Ghost is sent invisibly into our souls. "All the gifts of the Holy Ghost are distributed by Mary to those whom she chooses, whenever she wishes and as much as she wishes" says St. Bernardine of Siena.

The graces which the Holy Ghost pours down on us are due to the merits of Christ on Calvary; but in order that God may bestow them on the world, it is necessary that Mary should intervene. "By the communion of sorrows and of will between Christ and Mary," says Pius X, "she has deserved to become the dispenser of all the blessings which Jesus acquired for us by His blood" (Encyclical, February 2, 1904). "We may affirm," declares Leo XIII, "that by the will of God, nothing is given to us without Mary's mediation, in such a way that just as no one can approach the almighty Father but through His Son, so no one, so to speak, can approach Christ but through His mother" (Encycl., Sept. 22, 1891).

It is essential that Mary should constantly intercede for each one of us. This she does, relying on the blood of Christ by whom she was herself saved, and who alone

saves us. This actual intervention of Mary plays a preponderating part in the salvation of the world. It is important that we should realize this, and it is the object of the feast of Mary Mediatrix of all graces. [pp. 963 (18–19).]
185 Pope John Paul II repeatedly observed in the *Man and Woman He Created Them: A Theology of the Body* that the creation was also in every sense a sacrament. The creation was effected by a transforming *logos*.
186 *S.T.*, I–II, Q. 113, Art. 7, Ad 5.

APPENDIX EIGHT

The Future of Humanity, Etc.

THE FOLLOWING FOUR INITIATIVES are mentioned by Stephen Hawking et al. in his recent "Transcendence" paper,[187] introduced as follows:

> If a superior alien civilisation sent us a message saying, "We'll arrive in a few decades," would we just reply, "OK, call us when you get here—we'll leave the lights on"? Probably not—but this is more or less what is happening with AI. Although we are facing potentially the best or worst thing to happen to humanity in history, little serious research is devoted to these issues outside non-profit institutes such as the Cambridge Centre for the Study of Existential Risk, the Future of Humanity Institute, the Machine Intelligence Research Institute, and the Future of Life Institute. All of us should ask ourselves what we can do now to improve the chances of reaping the benefits and avoiding the risks.

Cambridge Centre for the Study of Existential Risk (Cambridge, UK)
www.cser.ac.uk

Modern science is well-acquainted with the idea of natural risks, such as asteroid impacts or extreme volcanic events, that might threaten our species as a whole. It is also a familiar idea that we ourselves may threaten our own existence, as a consequence of our technology and science. Such home-grown "existential risk"—the threat of global nuclear war, and of possible extreme effects of anthropogenic climate change—has been with us for several decades.

However, it is a comparatively new idea that developing technologies might lead—perhaps accidentally, and perhaps very rapidly, once a certain point is reached—to direct, extinction-level threats to our species. Such concerns have been expressed about artificial intelligence (AI), biotechnology, and nanotechnology, for example.

Future of Humanity Institute (Oxford, UK)
fhi.ox.ac.uk (closed April 2024)

The Future of Humanity Institute is a leading research centre looking at big-picture questions for human civilization. The last few centuries have seen tremendous change, and this century might transform the human condition in even more fundamental ways. Using the tools of mathematics, philosophy, and science, we explore the risks and opportunities that will arise from technological change, weigh ethical dilemmas, and evaluate global priorities. Our goal is to clarify the choices that will shape humanity's long-term future.

Machine Intelligence Research Institute (Berkeley, CA)
intelligence.org/2014/04/20/why-miri

The machine intelligence research institute (MIRI) was founded in 2000 on the premise that creating smarter-than-human artificial intelligence with a positive impact—"Friendly AI"—might be a particularly efficient way to do as much good as possible.

First, because future people vastly outnumber presently existing people, we think that "From a global perspective, what matters most (in expectation) is that we do what is best (in expectation) for the general trajectory along which our descendants develop over the coming millions, billions, and trillions of years." (See Nick Beckstead's *On the Overwhelming Importance of Shaping the Far Future*.)

Second, as an empirical matter, we think that smarter-than-human AI is humanity's most significant point of leverage on that "general trajectory along which our descendants develop." If we handle advanced AI wisely, it could produce tremendous goods which endure for billions of years. If we handle advanced AI poorly, it could render humanity extinct. No other future development has more upside or downside. (See Nick Bostrom's *Superintelligence: Paths, Dangers, Strategies*.)

Third, we think that Friendly AI research is tractable, urgent, and uncrowded.

Future Life Institute (Miami, FL)
futurelifeinstitute.org/2013/1preview.html

Education in these methods can multiply a person's freedom and range of choices, opening a gateway to higher quality future lives, and also a channel for positive change today.

New Adventure

Exciting new scientific advances are making it possible for spiritual beings to take charge of our future and shape our larger destiny. Awakened individuals who want to improve their upcoming lives can become pioneers who embrace the future and boldly strike out for new adventure. Entirely new kinds of future lives can be created by the scientific application of new methods and discoveries which optimize a person's reincarnation skills.

Note

187   https://www.independent.co.uk/news/science/stephen-hawking-transcendence-looks-at-the-implications-of-artificial-intelligence-but-are-we-taking-ai-seriously-enough-9313474.html

Ed. note (Andrew McLuhan): Hawking's paper was published January 1, 2014.

1. Conscious Creation

- Human beings can *accelerate our conscious evolution* through the intelligent design of future lives.

2. Freedom of Choice

- There is a much *broader array of choices* for our future lifetimes than previously imagined.

3. Intelligent Decisions

- We can make *intelligent decisions* in our selections for upcoming lifetimes by educating ourselves in the wide range of options that are actually available.

4. Trans-Life Psychology

- A new cognitive science called *trans-life psychology* enables human beings to deliberately create our future lives.

5. Trans-Life Memory

- Trans-life psychology has its foundations in a new *trans-life memory science*, which provides the scientific basis for ensuring that learning done today can travel with us into the future.

6. Spiritual Chemistry

- Trans-life memory science is supported by a new *spiritual chemistry*, whose axioms and formulas reveal fundamental laws governing the relationship between spirit and the physical universe.

(HAPPILY EVER) AFTERWORD

MARSHALL MCLUHAN WAS A self-described explorer, and he discovered a great deal in his lifetime. Ranging over vast intellectual territory, much of his work was undeveloped or half-finished, or otherwise never made it into print. His eldest son, Eric McLuhan (my father), followed him, and in some cases, Eric fully investigated issues that Marshall initially unearthed.

In *Understanding Media: The Extensions of Man* (MIT Press, 1964) and elsewhere, Marshall uses the term *sensus communis*, but nowhere does he take much time to explain what it means or why it matters. Here, in *The Sensus Communis, Synesthesia, and the Soul*, Eric has taken on that task.

My father taught me that a teacher's job is to save students' time, and in *The Sensus Communis* he has gone to Odyssean lengths to research and develop this "odd-essay" (as he called it). Originally, it wasn't supposed to be full book; as Eric notes, "I expected that... it would not take more than a dozen pages or so" to write a detailed note regarding the *sensus communis*.

But my father was a rigorous man, and he quickly uncovered great depth in the concept that had to be explored and resolved. The end result is a compelling case for how, individually and collectively, we've lost our holistic sensibilities and why it's so vital that we regain our *sensus communis*.

Despite this being a work of great detail, Eric nonetheless believed it was just the beginning and called the book "a sort of prologue or a set of notes to aid in beginning that longer, proper study." Unfortunately, he never had the opportunity to continue his investigation—he passed away three short years after *The Sensus Communis* was first published in 2015.

Marshall and Eric McLuhan had a singular relationship as father and son, and also as colleagues. It's often hard to tell where one's thinking began and the other's ended. I don't feel that my father was ever really given enough credit—it's just as well he didn't care about credit but about the work at hand. This essay is certainly a unique contribution to the McLuhan canon, and entirely to his credit.

A decade after first appearing in print, the core arguments in this book feel as vital as ever, as it threads our many senses through biology, technology, theology, and metaphysics. So vital that *The Sensus Communis* is released here as the first book under the McLuhan Institute Books imprint. Aside from a few small changes—swapping endnotes for footnotes, and a few very minor editorial and typographical tweaks—the book appears as it was originally conceived by Eric.

It is an unexpected journey to follow my grandfather and father, to build for their legacy a home for the twenty-first century and beyond. To that end, in loving memory and in recognition of Eric McLuhan's remarkable scholarship and dedication to the work, I'm pleased to bring *The Sensus Communis* back into a contemporary discourse to which it has so much to contribute.

Andrew McLuhan
Bloomfield, Ontario, 2025

BIBLIOGRAPHY

Alighieri, Dante. *Literary Criticism of Dante Alighieri.* Tr. And ed. Robert S. Haller. Lincoln, NB: University of Nebraska Press, 1973.

Aquinas, St. Thomas. *Summa Theologica.* In five vols. Notre Dame, in: Christian classics, 1948. Dominican translation, 1948, by Benziger Bros.; rpt. 1981 by Christian classics.

Aristotle. *On the Soul, Parva Naturalia, On Breath.* Loeb classical library. Tr. W. S. Hett. Cambridge, MA: Harvard University Press; London: William Heinemann, 1957.

Bloom, Harold. *The Western Canon: The Books and School of the Ages.* New York: Harcourt Brace & Company, 1994.

Booth, David. *Reading Doesn't Matter Anymore: Shattering the Myths of Literacy.* Markham, ON: Pembroke Publishers, 2006; Portland, ME: Stenhouse Publishers, 2006.

Canetti, Elias. *Crowds and Power.* Tr. Carol Stewart. London: Victor Gollancz, 1962; New York: Viking, 1963; New York: Penguin Books, 1973; rpt. Peregrine Books, 1987.

Carpenter, Edmund Snow. *Oh, What a Blow That Phantom Gave Me!* New York: Henry Holt & Company, 1973.

Cicero. *De Oratore.* Loeb Classical Library, vols. III, IV. Vol.

III, Books 1, 2. Tr. E. W. Sutton and H. Rackham. Cambridge, MA: Harvard University Press; London: William Heinemann, 1967. Vol. III, *De Oratore* Book 3; *De Fato; Paradoxa Stoicorum; Partitiones Oratoriae.* Tr. H. Rackham. Cambridge, MA: Harvard University Press; London: William Heinemann, 1968.

Cytowic, Richard E. *The Man Who Tasted Shapes: A Bizarre Medical Mystery Offers Revolutionary Insights into Emotions, Reasoning, and Consciousness.* New York: G. P. Putnam's Sons, 1993.

de Lubac, Henri. *Catholicism: Christ and the Common Destiny of Man.* Tr. Sheppard, Lancelot C., and Sr. Elizabeth Englund, OCD. San Francisco: Ignatius Press, 1988.

_____. *Exégèse médiévale: les quatre sens de l'écriture.* In four vols. Paris: Éditions Montaigne. Vol. I, 1959; vol. II, 1959; vol. III, 1961; vol. IV, 1964.

_____. *Medieval Exegesis: The Four Senses of Scripture.* Vol. I. Tr. mark Sebanc, 1998. Vol. II. Tr. E. M. Macierowski, 2000. Vol. III. Tr. E. M. Macierowski, 2009. Grand Rapids, MI: William B. Eerdmans; Edinburgh, Scotland: T&T Clark.

_____. *Paradoxes of Faith.* San Francisco: Ignatius Press, 1987.

Deveraux, G. "An Unusual Audio-motor Synesthesia in an Adolescent." *Psychiatric Quarterly* 40(3), 1966: 459–71.

Edwards, Paul, ed. *The Encyclopedia of Philosophy.* New York: Collier Macmillan, 1967; rpt. 1972.

Eliot, T. S. *To Criticize the Critic: Eight Essays on Literature and Education.* New York: Farrar, Straus & Giroux, 1965.

_____. *Four Quartets.* (The whole variously published and collected.) *Collected Poems 1909–1962.* London: Faber and Faber, 1963, pp. 187–223. Each of the four constituent poems was published separately as it was finished: "Burnt Norton" in 1935; "East Coker" in 1940; "The Dry Salvages" in 1941; "Little Gidding" in 1942.

―――――――. "Hamlet and his Problems." in *The Sacred Wood: Essays on Poetry and Criticism*. London: Methuen & co., 1920; New York: Alfred A. Knopf, 1921; New York: Barnes & Noble, 1960.

―――――――. "The Music of Poetry." In *On Poetry and Poets*. New York: The Noonday Press / Farrar, Straus & Cudahy, 1961.

―――――――. *On Poetry and Poets*. New York: Farrar, Straus & Cudahy / The Noonday Press, 1943, ... 1961.

―――――――. *The Use of Poetry & the Use of Criticism: Studies in the Relation of Criticism to Poetry in England*. London: Faber and Faber, 1933; rpt. 1959.

Ellul, Jacques. *Propaganda: The Formation of Men's Attitudes*. New York: Vintage Books, 1973.

Francis, Pope. *The Light of Faith (Lumen Fidei)*. Liberia Editrice Vaticana / San Francisco: Ignatius Press, 2013.

Gombrich, Sir Ernst H. *Art and Illusion: A Study in the Psychology of Pictorial Realism*. New York: Pantheon Books, 1960.

Gilson, Étienne. *The Christian Philosophy of St. Thomas Aquinas*. Tr. Lawrence K. Shook, CSB. Notre Dame, IN: University of Notre Dame Press, 1956; rpt. 2010.

Havelock, Eric. *Preface to Plato*. Cambridge, MA: Harvard University Press, 1963.

John Paul II, Pope. *Crossing the Threshold of Hope*. Td. Vittorio Messori. Milan: Arnoldo Mondadori Editiore. Toronto: Alfred A. Knopf, 1994.

―――――――. *Man and Woman He Created Them: A Theology of the Body*. Boston: Pauline Books & Media, 2006.

_____. *Redemptor Hominis*. Rome: Libreria Editrice Vaticana, 1979.

_____. *Sources of Renewal: The Implementation of the Second Vatican Council*. San Francisco: harper & row, 1980.

_____. *Veritatis Splendor*. London: Catholic Truth Society/Dublin: Veritatis Publications, 1993.

Lanham, Richard. *A Handlist of Rhetorical Terms*. 2nd ed. Berkeley/ Los Angeles/Oxford: University of California Press, 1991.

Lasch, Christopher. *The Minimal Self: Psychic Survival in Troubled Times*. New York and London: W. W. Norton, 1984.

Lewis, Wyndham. *The Art of Being Ruled*. London: Chatto & Windus, 1926; rpt. Santa Rosa, CA: Black Sparrow Press, 1989.

_____. *Doom of Youth*. New York: Robert m. McBride and co., 1932; rpt., New York: Haskell House, 1973.

_____. *The Enemy: A Review of Art and Literature*, Edited and Illustrated by Wyndham Lewis, no. 1 (January 1927; rpt. Santa Rosa, CA: Black Sparrow Press, 1994.

Lusseyran, Jacques. *Et la lumière fut*. Paris: la Table ronde, 1953). *And There Was Light*. Tr. from the French by Elizabeth Cameron. Boston and Toronto: Little, Brown and Company, 1963.

McLuhan, Eric, "Aristotle's Media War." © 2014. A version of this essay appeared as "Aristotle's Theory of communication" in McLuhan, Eric, and Marshall McLuhan. *Theories of Communication*. New York: Peter Lang, 2011, pp. 189–92.

_____. "Communication Arts in the Ancient World" © 2009; rev., 2014. This essay, much abbreviated, appeared in McLuhan, Eric, and Marshall McLuhan. *Theories of Communication*. New York: Peter Lang, 2011, p. 225.

———. "On Formal Cause." *Explorations in Media Ecology*, 4 (3–4), December 2005: 181–210.

McLuhan, Marshall. *The Gutenberg Galaxy: The Making of Typographic Man*. Toronto: University of Toronto Press, 1962.

———. *Understanding Media: The Extensions of Man*. New York: McGraw-Hill, 1964.

McLuhan, Marshall, and Eric McLuhan. *Laws of Media: The New Science*. Toronto: University of Toronto Press, 1988.

McLuhan, Marshall, and Harley Parker. *Through the Vanishing Point: Space in Poetry and Painting*. New York: Harper & Row, 1968.

Newman, J. K. *Augustus and the New Poetry*. Bruxelles-Berchem: Latomus, Revue d'Études Latines, 1967.

Ohler, Jason. *Digital Storytelling in the Classroom: New Media Pathways to Literacy, Learning and Creativity*. Thousand Oaks, CA: Corwin Press, 2008.

Paulos, J. A. *Innumeracy: Mathematical Illiteracy and its Consequences*. New York: Hill and Wang, 1988.

Peacham, Henry. *The Garden of Eloquence* (1577). Reproduced in part in Willard R. Espy. *The Garden of Eloquence: A Rhetorical Bestiary*. Including portions of the first *Garden of Eloquence* by Henry Peacham. New York: Harper & Row, 1983.

Postman, Neil. *The Disappearance of Childhood*. New York: Vintage Books, 1982.

Pound, Ezra. *ABC of Reading*. New York: New Directions, 1960.

Puttenham, George. *The Arte of English Poesie* (sixteenth century). Tds. Gladys Doidge Willcock and Alice Walker. Cambridge: at the University Press, 1936; rpt. 1970.

Quintilian. *Institutio Oratoria*. Loeb Classical Library. In four vols. Tr. H. T. Butler. Vol. I, Book 1. Cambridge, MA: Harvard University Press; London: William Heinemann, 1963.

Ratzinger, Joseph Cardinal. *The Ratzinger Report: An Exclusive Interview on the State of the Church.* Tr. Attanasio, Salvator, and Graham Harrison. San Francisco: Ignatius Press, 1985.

Sanders, Barry. *A Is for Ox: The Collapse of Literacy and the Rise of Violence in an Electronic Age.* New York: Random House/ Vintage Books, 1994.

Shannon, Claude Elwood, and Warren Weaver. *The Mathematical Theory of Communication.* Champaign, IL: University of Illinois Press, 1963.

Varro, Marcus T. *De Lingua Latina.* Loeb Classical Library. In two vols. Tr. Roland G. Kent. Vol. I, Books 5–7. Cambridge, MA: Harvard university Press; London: William Heinemann, 1938. rev. And rpt. 1951. Vol. II, Books 8–10, and Fragments. Cambridge, MA: Harvard University Press, and London: William Heinemann, 1938. rev. And rpt. 1951; rpt. 2006.

Waldstein, Michael. *Introduction to Man and Woman He Created Them: A Theology of the Body*, by Pope John Paul II. Boston: Pauline Books & Media, 2006.

West, Diana. *The Death of the Grown-Up: How America's Arrested Development Is Bringing Down Western Civilization.* New York: St. Martin's Press, 2007.

Wolf, Maryanne. *Proust and the Squid: The Story and Science of the Reading Brain.* New York: HarperCollins, 2007.

Yeats, W. B. "Sailing to Byzantium." in *Collected Poems of W. B. Yeats.* London, Melbourne; Toronto: Macmillan, 1967, pp. 217–18.

ERIC MCLUHAN (1942–2018) WAS a renowned literary and communications theorist. He is the author of eighteen books, including *Cynic Satire*, *The Human Equation* series (written with mime artist Wayne Constantineau), and *Theories of Communication*. He also co-authored essays and books with Marshall McLuhan, including *Media and Formal Cause* and *Laws of Media: The New Science*.

Printed by Imprimerie Gauvin
Gatineau, Québec